M000213591

I read them last night and today and I think you have a really wise, warm, funny voice. It (your writing) has a great, natural quality to it—and that's not easy to do.

—Andy Ward, *Random House*

Stories are what comprise a life. This collection represents windows into a lifetime of friends, family, events, happenings. They're simple stories on the surface but have a deeper meaning. We look in a window and see one view but there is always more once we go inside. What does an old family picture truly reveal? What do we learn about a best friend's mother who died too young. Warrington's stories are well written and powerful. They capture the nuances, wisdom, surprises, inspiration, and losses related to experiences in her life that we can relate to in our own.

—Sybil K. Goldman, *Georgetown University*

Freda Warrington's work is impressive. It has a mystical, almost Biblical quality. She recreates the past with exactitude while using it to leverage our understanding of the present. To experience her writing is to know everything about the inequity of longing and loss. But her stream of prose catches us in eddies of hope, and therein lies all the difference.

—David Colman, *writer, editor, publisher*

"Elixir For Auntie" as memoir and literature does a nice job of joining the woman, your love for her, and the education death imparts. It's a classic story, but you tell it really well. For me "Golden Box of Bones" resonates deeply as it contrasts the overscheduled Jew walking into the depths of the thoughtful, spiritual hospital/church…a little like the script of a softer, gentler Twilight Zone episode.

—Alfred Spector, *VP of Research and Special Initiatives, Google*

I loved your "Dead Wall" essay. How great it is that you have so much knowledge about all those faces from the past and that they emerge as real people to whom you can relate. The information at the end is horrendous. You write in a most interesting way…vividly and with a rich choice of words.

—Sylvia Feinburg, *Professor Emerita, Tufts University*

Since you are truly the WORLD'S CHAMPION at friendship, I've been uniquely blessed. Your memoir about our mothers and our growing up together with mothers who created happy homes that were open and welcoming has touched me beyond anything I've experienced in a long time. Thank you for honoring our mothers.

—Joyce Radochia,

(the Joy in "The Samovar and The Egg") Renaissance Woman

I immensely enjoyed reading "Shattered." In particular, the paragraph that begins "My stuff" provoked a "wow…I love this!" response in me. It is written beautifully, and I related to it so much—making sense as it did as to why I'm attached to things that really mean so little to anyone else—and even legitimizing those attachments. I loved the by-play and various responses from family and friends…very funny.

—Dianne Cooper, *MA, MFCC*

I read your "Dead Wall Revelation" and cried for your family and mine. I was so young when Mom died and didn't know enough or care enough to get more details. Our family pictures were destroyed in an unexpected flood when I was a little one. There's no one left now to ask about what happened. I'm glad your mother could tell you and felt I was there when she did.

—Carol Appelbaum, *reader, CASA volunteer*

"Doppelganger" is really fun—a VERY quirky, perceptive and unusual piece of writing, and it's fascinating to read your take on this!

—The Other Freda Warrington, *author of* A Taste of Blood Wine *and dozens of fantasy and vampire novels*

I'm among the most appreciative in your audience for your writing. I know you have many admirers, but please do consider me at the top of the list. Your choice of words, rhythm and ability to draw such a detailed picture, as well as your deep understanding of the human condition bring your subjects vividly to life, no matter how long or short an individual piece might be.

—Phyllis Jansen, *reader and Vassar classmate*

I am so deeply moved after reading "The Samovar and the Egg." I cannot find the words. Your piece has come to me at a time when I have been immersed in finding my own mother, as I'm losing a friend. I sat down to a late breakfast, early lunch of a warm egg salad sandwich and your writing as my company. Oh my, Freda, it is funny and fascinating and explores a wealth of emotions and with such detail. And it is both gentle and wise and curious. How can this all be at the same time? Indeed, dear lady, you are a storyteller, a fine one indeed.

—Frannie Oates, *Storyteller*

"Dead Wall Revelation" is an amazing story that must be told. This story is so detailed, rich and painful. I admire you for telling it.

—Laurie Everett, *Senior Associate Director of Communications, Resource Development at MIT*

Bardolf & Company

LISTEN TO THE LIGHT
Stories of Interruptions, Intersections and Insights

ISBN 978-1-938842-33-7

Copyright © 2017 by Freda S. Warrington

All rights reserved by the copyright holder. The scanning, uploading and
distribution of this book without permission is a theft of the author's intellectual
property. No part of this book may be used or reproduced in any form or by
any electronic or mechanical means, including information storage and retrieval
systems, without permission in writing from the author. For any use of material
from this book (other than for review purposes), please contact the author via the
publisher' address below. Thank you for your support of the author's rights.

Published by Bardolf & Company
5430 Colewood Pl.
Sarasota, FL 34232
941-232-0113
www.bardolfandcompany.com

To My Grandchildren
Camryn, Kaylee, Nicholas, Mia, Rocco and Matteo

LISTEN TO THE LIGHT

Stories of Interruptions, Intersections and Insights

Freda S. Warrington

Bardolf & Company
Sarasota, Florida

Contents

Preface *2*

Introduction *5*

Dead Wall Revelation *6*

A Dream Come True *22*

The Samovar and The Egg *26*

Shiva Candle Skeptic *40*

The Blintz as Metaphor *46*

A Golden Box of Bones *53*

Shattered *60*

Of All Sad Words… *68*

The Winter of the Scarf *80*

One Door Closes *87*

Dopplegangers *91*

Inevitable? *95*

Thank You, Warden *99*

Another Man's Treasure *106*

Elixir for Auntie *122*

Dying As a Complication of Living *129*

Bought With Butter *137*

Acknowledgments *173*

Preface

Some people think of life as a journey, a metaphor implying a destination or direction no matter how circuitous. And for some people there is a presumptuous attempt to follow a carefully constructed plan for the trip. A young woman might decide to attend graduate school, join a hedge fund, get rich and then think about a proper marriage or her biological time clock. A young man might set his sights on finding Mr. or Ms. Right and establishing a family, whether it's during high school or later in life. The young especially don't know yet that plans count for little. The rest of us keep hoping or praying for the best.

The twists, turns, ups and downs of our lives make for excitement or terror or boredom. That we even dare step foot outside the safety of our homes is a tribute to a courageous human spirit, since we're all heading ultimately toward the same end. As dark as this seems, an embracing of the interruptions and intersections that come upon us, unplanned and when least expected, lead us toward insight and maybe even wisdom.

We're spun around when our mothers or fathers die, for who else will ever love us as well; we may have a good laugh or cry when we look in the mirror; we're struck by fear when we don't know where to turn for advice. We feel rich with new life when a grandchild is born; we're lost when we're flooded out; we become believers when a miraculous dream becomes a reality; we're proud when we adopt a truth as our own even though many others already know it. We're re-invigorated by the simplest things such as a phone call, and at other times we're overwhelmed just thinking about a busy day to come. A family member disappoints us with her greed and thoughtlessness and then a stranger pops out from nowhere to gift us with a long lost family heirloom instead of selling it for personal gain.

If insight manages to work its way into our lives, there's a good chance we can exit this world without regret and perhaps with gratitude. Every experience does not need to be overanalyzed for nuance or deconstructed in a frantic quest. But, meaning does exist and is there for the taking. My own experiences with interruptions and intersections have brought me both pleasure and pain and, I like to believe, a degree of insight. I share these stories with my readers knowing full well that their personal stories of interruptions, intersections and insights may well be more curious or more miraculous than my own and ripe for the plucking.

—*Freda S. Warrington*
 January 2017
 Sarasota, Florida

Freda S. Warrington

Introduction

In acquiring objects, the collector sees through them to the past, and the act of collecting can feel something like redemption. Assembling the collection into a magic circle, the collector breathes life into the objects and in so doing, he renews his own existence, as well as theirs. The act of fixing each object in place offers collectors "the most profound enchantment," even a sense of omniscience, allowing them to peer through the objects deep into the worlds through which they have traveled.

The above is Walter Benjamin's description of the archivist and book collector's passion. His words have illuminated a way for me to understand my personal drive to collect my stories. The notion of "fixing" the event, the person, the occasion, the artifact into place has been not only comforting but also instructive. The written words have become the glue and the stories cannot escape.

It has been my passion to collect and sort, as Benjamin describes, the chaos of my memories.

Dead Wall Revelation

My 89-year-old mother cried as she accidentally surrendered a detail of the family's past. She'd squirreled away the scrap in some dark recess, but now she dropped it to land where it might. As I walk toward my den with its Dead Wall of photographs, home now to many I've loved, I wonder why now? Am I finally old enough to have suffered sufficient

My grandfather Alter Karelitz with his family. In the foreground are his parents, Rabbi Aaron Baruch Karelitz and Shayna Gordon Karelitz

personal pain that Mother can trust me enough to share in hers? Or was it simply and finally her need to lighten a burden grown too heavy?

Yesterday the superficial truth of the photographs of the family from the Old Country, attesting only to their existence, was quite acceptable to me. And, I must confess that yesterday I was careless enough to believe that being posted on my Dead Wall was honor enough for my lost family. Today, though, as I look at my great grandparents and great aunts in their formal pose, my eyes are open fully to them as living, breathing and, yes, dying people. I'm seeing the same old photographs but am compelled to acknowledge the complexities of their lives and the brutality of their deaths. Unlike yesterday I now believe there was meaning to their lives and deaths.

◄◉

It is June 1934 and my great-grandmother, Shayna Gordon Karelitz, sits beside my great grandfather, Aaron Baruch Karelitz. The elderly couple is smiling slightly, no doubt pleased to welcome home to Baltrimanz, Lithuania[1] an honored guest, their son, Alter, who stands at the center of the photograph. Alter has come a long way from Malden, Massachusetts on the Holland America Line and is focused on his serious mission.

Shayna dotes on her Alter, never forgetting how fortunate she is to have him in this world. She recalls how she'd cheated the dybbuks who had stolen the life of her firstborn and threatened the life of the newborn. Rather than naming him after her

---

[1]Baltrimanz, Lithuania, a village not far from Kovno.

Max's nightmare (digging in Lithuanian field)

grandfather, Shayna was clever and named the baby, Alter, Old One, for such demons would have no use for an old man. Shayna was thinking outside the box of her shtetl back in July 1888 when she bravely gave birth to my grandfather by the light of a kerosene lamp in her damp stone and plaster cottage on Tartashe Gass in Alytus, Lithuania.

Nearly a half-century later and standing behind the white-haired Shayna and gray-bearded Aaron Baruch are their grown children, none of whom are smiling. The anxiety of uncertainty is present at the moment the shutter opens and then snaps closed. Wearing blouses of fabric so contemporary we'd expect to see them on a Macy's rack are Frumkeh and Blumah, the youngest of the three sisters. On the other side of their brother, Alter, stands Ruth married to Chaim Poliansky from Sasli, Poland. The couple had married on November 4, 1927 and when their wedding photograph was taken, it was mailed across the sea as a "forever memorial for Alter Karelitz and his family."

For that occasion Ruth wore her hair in a short bob with a stylish finger wave and had chosen a high necked and understated blouse. Chaim's starched white collar and carefully knotted necktie with a silk handkerchief peeking from his chest pocket reflected a man who was a dapper dresser. He and Ruth were both serious and seemed distracted in their wedding day photo although it was only 1927. As I attempt to conjure their feelings on what should have been the happiest day of their lives, I wonder if they suffered a chill from a premonition that theirs would be a short marriage. Might they have guessed their wedding photograph would be archivally framed on my Dead Wall, a relic worth its weight in gold, instead of collecting dust in an ordinary pile of attic ephemera?

During the photoshoot I imagine that Chaim complained to Ruth that the photographer was a robber, full of himself ever since he'd photographed Morris Gest, Baltrimanz' favorite son and a very big star from America on his first visit home since childhood. Chaim knew what austerity meant in spite of owning a good suit and a silk handkerchief.

Seven years later it's a cool June day in 1934 and time to gather the family for this photo op. Alter stands tall next to his three sisters in front of the same robber photographer who had cornered the village's photography market. Alter is disappointed that Max, the baby of the family, is missing from the family picture because of the high cost of passage from America. Yet, he's relieved, on the one hand, that Max is safe though, on the other, he's feeling guilty that Max must fill and deliver Alter's work orders in addition to his own.

The family chats about the absent Max, their young prince. They're not amused as they recall the feisty kid of 14, confident of his immortality, as he slipped out of the village in 1922 to make his way to Berlin, then Antwerp and onto the Red Star Line to New York. Along with his papers and documents folded in a brown leather valise and secured by a heavy cotton strap, Max packed a change of clothes and a few photos. Today his passport and visas are secure in my possession though crumbling further each time I scour them for missed information.

Chaim interrupts Alter's apprehensive thinking with a quiet grumble behind Ruth's back about paying for the photographer's fancy new tripod. Alter doesn't answer because he's exhausted from all the arguing and pleading as he's tried to sell Blumah and the rest of the family on her departure from Lithuania. He has meticulously laid out a best-case scenario. On the plus side, she'll be treasured by the young family he's created in America as the lone auntie from his side of the family. As for the worst-case scenario? The future is uncertain in Lithuania. That is Alter's best guess.

I now know that Alter was entirely wrong because the future was certain. But Alter has learned to speak kindly of others, to reject gossip, and to look on the bright side.

Shayna asks Alter once more to repeat his big ideas. "Tell me your plans, son." And in his plans, his grand plans, he promises his mother that one by one, or two by two, he'll rescue the family from the powdery dirt and poverty of Baltrimanz. While the streets of Malden, Massachusetts are not paved with gold, opportunity is everywhere. Cousins are working in factories owned by righteous

Jews like his close friend and next door neighbor, Mr. Feuerstein, of Malden Mills.

As the photographer adjusts the final configuration with the old folks in high backed chairs, Chaim's right arm resting on the back of his father-in-law's chair and Frumkeh's left arm a mirror image on the back of her mother's chair, Alter wonders how he'll break the news to Max that he hasn't presented a convincing enough argument to their little sister, Blumah. Will Max blame him for coming up short in his sales pitch? Will Max comprehend Blumah›s unwillingness to leave Lithuania and their elderly parents to embrace the beloved new country? Will he not curse Blumah's continued faith in Yahweh in spite of theft, conscriptions, and pogroms?

As an incentive for his sister, Alter describes the Cunard ship, Berengaria, that would carry them to America. He tells Blumah about its elegant carpeted library, glorious public bathrooms with tubs of fresh green water, and the availability of any food she would want, even oranges, and all for a nickel tip to the steward. "And don't forget your bathing suit," Alter says. "The swimming pool is 100 feet long!"

Blumah is still not convinced and so with one last appeal, Alter offers up his Graham Paige. He promises to teach her to brake smoothly and use her left hand to signal turns. But Blumah answers in a clear voice saying that the Baltrimanz trolley or even a droshky can transport her to the beauty parlor without threatening her life. His machine races at breakneck speeds and spews dirty fumes while exploding like gunshots. Having grown up in the Talmudic world of her scholarly father and the kabalistic world of her mother, Blumah believes there is something profane, never mind unsafe, about a complex assemblage of gears, wheels, and tanks. Although she knows in her heart that Alter means well, her life is here, yes right here, in this dusty village, alongside her family and the old folks who depend on her. She wishes Alter would quit arguing and leave well enough alone. He always was argumentative, she recalls, and even as a little boy, he had big plans. He took on the role of the droshky driver while she and her sisters were reduced to his towing nags.

Alter is not listening to Chaim's complaints about the photographer as he envisions his embarkation day next week when he'll sail to safety in international waters. He instinctively pats his waist where folded neatly into a secret pocket is enough currency for Blumah's passage to America. Although he's a poor man, a peddler who sells garments and dishes, he's proud to have saved enough money for a one-way ticket for his little sister.

But now Alter is worn down after frequent and heated discussions have peppered the entire week, before and after every meal, after morning prayers and even on Shabbos. Her decision is final. Fear of the unknown in America makes Blumah's stomach knot up for she's not a risk-taker.

Alter is puzzled that Blumah's decision to stay or to leave is not an especially wrenching one even after his description of his harrowing journey to Lithuania: the German security, the near arrest and confiscation of his savings, and the borders that were nearly impervious.

Yet, Blumah still holds no second thoughts and Alter is beginning to accept that he'll be traveling home alone, sunning himself on a lower deck on the Cunard's R.M.S. Berengaria, smiling for yet another camera and swallowing fears that "things" will get worse. His carefully crafted plans have been for nothing and his former optimism has now shifted 180 degrees to frustration and disappointment.

He's tried his best to describe to his family the nearly impossible travel conditions in Europe. He's warned them repeatedly as he related his terror on the streets of Berlin. The family listens, nods, while pretending to understand but does not change its mind even though Alter demonstrated how everyone on the street was Heil Hitlering, how the lightning police shouted, "Put up your arm!" before he was dragged into detention at the local station.

Alter continued his story and his mother trembled with a mixture of awe and disbelief when she heard how Alter talked his way out of police headquarters declaring his innocence by virtue of his American citizenship. And then she covered her mouth with her work-worn hand when Alter told of another interrogation at the border crossing where he was ordered to declare all valuables. Knowing that Blumah's passage money would be confiscated, Alter undertook the biggest risk of his life, more frightening than passing on a one lane country road at Crystal Lake and more dangerous than putting all his financial eggs in one peddler's basket. He lied to the authorities.

Although educated at a gymnasium and fluent in eight languages including German, Alter pretended not to understand the command and shrugged his shoulders with eyebrows raised in dismay. He appeared confused enough to be harmless and managed to squirm into Lithuania.

By the time he arrived in Baltrimanz, his hopes were high that he could accomplish his mission as the pressured Nazi fingerprints on his arm faded. He felt like he was on the Revere Beach roller coaster where from the top swell he could see everything below as he screamed downward into a near free fall. He knew that all the hugs and kisses, tsimmes and taiglach, along with non-stop well wishers did not reflect the truth of the times.

✺

The photographer packs up his new tripod and camera while the Karelitz family ambles out of its geometry. Alter's empty feelings are tricking him into believing he's hungry or perhaps lonely for his wife, Molly, and their children, Ethel and Leon. Sandwiched together, these feelings make for an unbearably sad departure from Baltrimanz, although Alter has no concrete knowledge that he will not see his family again. Even he cannot conceive of a further crescendo of cruelty, any rules more comprehensive or bitter than exist today at the manned border stations, any demands tougher than the polished leather of the police boots, or any voices more strident than those of the fanatics whose Heil Hitlers echo off the brick buildings and cobblestone streets of Berlin.

The nausea he's experiencing on Sunday, July 22, 1934 continues over the next five days. He thinks it's due to the ship speeding though rough seas, but perhaps it's a free floating and malevolent anxiety that Alter can't quite name.

✺

Until the war ends and June 10, 1945 arrives, Alter will not know with certainty that his parents, sisters, brother-in-law, cousins, aunts and uncles have all perished. When his brother, Max, now a supply sergeant in the U.S. Army and a most willing soldier, passes through a liberated Dachau, he questions one skeletal survivor after another.

"What do you know about the Karelitz family from Baltrimanz?" Either no one knows or no one has the heart to tell the earnest American soldier. Finally, Max is handed a copy of a typewritten speech by Dr. Z. Grinberg and delivered at the Liberation Concert in Munich-Freiman.[2]

Max reads as fast as he can. "Different is the road, various are the stations of torture, different is the space of time, but there is one common thread of blood, torture, torment, humiliation, and undignified death." The good doctor wrote pages of details of the story that began the night of Sunday, June 22, 1941, four years before Max's arrival at the death camp. That was the night Dr. Grinberg heard shooting as the German army approached Kovno and headed toward an attack on the Soviet army. The peace in the village was interrupted and the radio warned repeatedly of reprisals. "For every German soldier killed, 100 Jews will be shot," Max reads. Thus began the methodical execution of the Baltrimanz villagers, the Karelitz family included, street by street, one by one and many at once whenever possible.

Max, by now an American patriot, a too-late liberator, tramps past the smokestacks of Dachau and on through the downed barbed wire. He sobs until he can no longer stand upright.

[2] See full text of Dr. Grinberg Speech at www.fredaswarrington.com

❦

What no one in our family knew until August of 1946 when Cousin Adina arrived in America, fresh and raw from a displaced persons camp, was one important detail. It was a terrible bit of information, blight on the last straw. What she revealed to Max, Alter and his daughter, Ethel, my mother, married by then with three small children, was that the family had been forced to dig their own graves. The old Aaron Baruch, the young son-in-law, Chaim Poliansky, and maybe the women, sweated into the fresh dug dirt before they were shot to death above the holes and then shoveled bleeding into the ditches.

Mother's eyes filled with tears and her ruddy complexion turned to white as her guest whispered the words she could not bear to voice. Cousin Adina was wounded, scarred for her eternity, and unable to eat the simple lunch my mother had prepared.

Adina was one of the few survivors from our extended family. She explained her continued existence simply. "I am a chemist," she told Mother. Her husband was taken away and murdered, she said, and with a deep breath, she looked down into our tiny crib in the dining room where my newborn baby brother, Arthur, was fretting. Adina picked up the baby and told Mother, "I had a baby...once." She cradled Arthur gently as if weighing him and then eased him off to my mother's arms.

From her purse, she pulled out an envelope to slip to her cousin, Max. So he wouldn't forget his homeland. He opened it to find a nearly colorless photo postcard that he examined for an endless moment before tucking it into the pocket inside his jacket next to his heart. In the photo men were lined up digging holes in a field.

I was three years old and do not remember everyone's tears.

❧

I can hear Mother crying as we talk on the phone this morning while she reveals this terrible piece of news, learned from Adina in 1946, but concealed so as not to burden my siblings or me. She cannot, now or ever, bear the thought that her family, devoted and filled with love for the God of their fathers, ended their lives as grave-diggers.

Mother is now an 89 year old widow and the very last of her generation. Her eyes are cloudy with cataracts, her hearing is lost, her back is bent from tiny fractures, and her legs barely keep her mobile. I am her child of almost 62 years and my mother continues as my cheerleader even now as she accuses me with a catch in her young voice. "You are breaking my heart," she weeps. Feeling guilty and ruthless, I thank her from the bottom of my heart and assure her that this perverse fragment of information is important for me to know.

Without the entire authentic and rotten story, I tell Mother, my Dead Wall photos offer but a sanitized record of existence without describing for me, for my children or grandchildren, the truth of their lives that includes their deaths. I tell Mother how often we've seen beautiful yet useless, nameless old photos languishing in the dusty back room of an antique store. How many beloved parents and grandparents, uncles and aunts, have been left hanging pointlessly on a Dead Wall because keeping the secrets of their deaths trumps the facts of how they lived and died? Sadly and understandably, the need to protect oneself in combination with a degree of misplaced guilt creates an adhesion that fixes itself around the human heart unless, like Mother, one summons courage.

Now I've already broken my mother's heart by hearing her terrible secret. Yet I dare not tell her that she's unraveled the answer to the mystery photograph on my Dead Wall. I'd often wondered what was so special about this nearly pale old picture that was so precious to my great uncle Max. But as I hung up the telephone, it became clear. For the moment, I felt as if I'd solved the riddle of the Sphinx while unearthing the Dead Sea Scrolls from their cave. It felt just that momentous, this ability to connect mother's secret to a photograph that was significant to my great uncle Max and for which, by accident, I'd assumed guardianship.

This seemingly inconsequential artifact that stood prominently on his desk in a silver filigree frame had been transferred to me after his death. Did Max leave it on his desk as a reminder to keep his rage alive? Was it a reminder of the Lithuanian soil that absorbed the blood and bones of his mother, father and sisters? Or might the photo have provided him a perverse comfort? I will never know, but before he died, Max would tell me only that it was a picture from the Old Country. It alone survived intact unlike everything else in his house that had been fractured (and glued back together as the sun rose and his demons subsided) by the tornado that was Max's rage. His landlady had corroborated those monster nightmares that always ended with Max shredding a set of her sheets.

I pace myself as I write and remind myself to take a deep breath while my reality is quickly changing. The mystery photo in its fancy frame captures nine men in long sleeve shirts, suspenders, and caps as they stop for a moment while digging in a field. Seven men are standing in a line with scythes and shovels while two men are up to their waists in holes. Behind the men two horses graze quietly. As an afterthought, a pastel sunrise sky was washed on at the photography studio to herald a beautiful day. I hope mightily that those trenches and holes were to store potatoes through the winter.

⟪©

It's more than two decades since Max's death and oddly enough my character flaws of stubbornness and inertia have morphed into positive territory. My refusal to toss the photo into the trashcan reminds me to continue to trust my instincts that whispered to me of an important occasion. On that particular day, while the air smelled of recently turned dirt, a photographer, perhaps the same village robber with his camera on his not-so-new tripod, captured a record that would become a last testament to these men, maybe our family, who I pray believed in a heaven as they dug up the field. They paused for just a moment while the shutter opened and the image was imprinted.

⟪©

As I straighten the tilt of a few photos on my Dead Wall, I recall that yesterday the men in the photo were lined up in the field, resting after digging a potato hole and waiting for the women to call them in for a hearty breakfast of a little herring, some brown bread, and perhaps a square of lokshen. Today, Mother's secret has jolted my reality and she's unwittingly compelled me to record these details of plans gone awry.

The meaning of the lives and deaths of my family, the Karelitz family of Baltrimanz, has become apparent because of the mystery photo. Without discovering its story, I most certainly would have continued to shake my head in disbelief that human beings are capable of such despicable acts of cruelty. I would have continued to hand over to the great scholars and philosophers the task of wringing out some cosmic interpretations from this catastrophe of the Holocaust. Instead, my mother's personal act of courage, in spite of her physical limitations and emotional struggle, has preserved the story, beyond the facts of history. She has provided dignity and depth to the lives and deaths of our family including that of Blumah who would not leave her old parents.

A Dream Come True

My great grandfather, Rabbi Baruch Cohen, was an interpreter of dreams. It has been reported that people from all around Briansk, Poland visited him and brought along their mysterious visions and fearsome dybbuks. Rabbi Cohen provided clarity and hope in a world of pogroms and poverty. He allowed my mother to sit on his lap and play with his long red beard when he visited the family in New York City in the 1920s.

I t was a spring day in 1978 and our nine-year-old daughter was in the midst of her cartwheel stage. She'd outgrown her pigtails and plaid-shirted Holly (Land of the Lost) persona but had not yet entered her horse phase in which she got stuck. The afternoon was sunny and the neighborhood children, after taking a running start on our driveway, were throwing their bodies over and over like pinwheels onto one side of our front yard.

All the houses on Seven Oaks in Kingwood, Texas were different, but our front yards and walkways were the same except for a few minor discrepancies in lawn quality. St. Augustine grass, with its stubborn runners, was best suited to our soil and climate, although some homeowners were beset by chinch bugs that created larger or smaller brown patches. Other lawns suffered from fungus or sprinkler deficiencies, but for the men in the neighborhood, lawns were a unifying source of community. They bonded on weekends as they inspected each other's lawn problems and offered personal diagnoses. They enjoyed Aha moments after coffee-can-captures of pests and the spring spread of steaming, stinking bags of organic matter.

It was in and on this lawn after the manure had settled into the thick thatch that our children played. I kept my eye on them through the dining room curtains, and all went well until our daughter raced into the house crying, "Your ring's gone." The ring she was talking about was the gold ring with the pearl that she wasn't supposed to wear outdoors because it was too big for her finger and might get lost.

I hollered in frustration, "Go on back out and find it!"

My parents had given me the ring when I was twelve and I wore it through high school and college. Even though the nacre on the pearl had nearly worn off, I still loved the ring and was angry that our daughter had defied my order to leave the ring in her jewelry box.

All the children hunted on their hands and knees in the patch of lawn where they had been cartwheeling. They'd spent at least an hour searching when I thought of using my husband's new Sears Roebuck shop vac to suction the lawn. I attached a heavy-duty orange extension cord, found an electrical outlet and methodically began, on my hands and knees, to vacuum the lawn. I'd created a virtual grid and fully expected the gold ring to pop into the open mouth of the vac.

Several times husbands from this classic bedroom community stopped their cars on the way home from Houston. What was I up to now? Was I looking for a contact lens? A diamond earring? Would I wait, one smart alec asked, while he raced home to fetch his camera?

The ring didn't turn up and I had a bad attitude when I went back in the house to make dinner.

《❀

I had an especially restless night's sleep and woke up several times with a dream that the ring with the pearl was soaring high and landing on the other side of the lawn and close to the mailbox. Since the children hadn't been playing there, it never crossed my mind to vacuum that side of the lawn.

I forgot about the dream since I've always suffered from dreams that are completely unremarkable except for how ridiculous they are. I have swinging dreams when I'm going too high, falling and dropping dreams, horror dreams when my brakes fail or raging dreams when my husband tells me he's fallen in love with someone else. As soon as I wake up, the memory of my nonsensical dreams disappear to leave me in peace.

As usual, the next morning I packed lunch boxes with thermoses, peanut butter sandwiches and Hostess cupcakes. I added healthy roughage, carrot sticks, for them to throw in the trash. I double knotted my son's shoelaces and brushed and tied up my daughter's hair as gently as possible while she complained. We checked for the presence of any forgotten homework and then I walked the kids to our mailbox at the street and waved them off toward the community greenbelt that led to their school.

Rabbi Baruch Cohen,
Palestine, 1926

When I saw the mailbox, I recalled my dream but it was of no consequence. I pivoted to go toward the house and felt something hard, perhaps a rock under my shoe. I bent down to fish into the thick thatch of lawn. I saw nothing but felt it and like a Liveable Forest Houdini, I pulled the lost ring from beneath the runners of the St. Augustine directly beneath my shoe. Voila! With two fingers I held it up to the morning light, stunned to think the ring had landed on the other side of the lawn. What were the chances, I wondered, that I would stand on top of it or feel it through the thick sole of my running shoe?

It's now more than thirty years since the event, and I've finally accepted it as a small miracle rather than a simple confluence of mathematical combinations. I've mounted the ring on red velvet in a shadow box as a reminder for when I feel let down, jaded, cynical, or believe I've seen it all. And now, the stories of my great grandfather's interpretive genius are no longer simply sweet, empty folktales about impoverished shtetl dwellers looking for justice or hope or answers.

Maybe one ought to listen to one's dreams, wait for the light and then look around.

The Samovar and the Egg

It was 1946 and three year old Freyde, a name which happens to mean Joy in Yiddish, moved with her family to a new house, a single family house with an elm tree in the backyard and a maple tree in front. A white picket fence enclosed the front yard but was interrupted by an archway that reminded her mother, Etta, of the chuppa on her wedding day.

Before this happy day Freyde's mother, an attorney, and her father, Asher, the proprietor of the Park Pharmacy, had been quietly barred from buying a house in that town because it was suspected that they were Jewish. They'd been seen walking to the little shul on Sylvia Street. It was true, that Asher sometimes prayed with phylacteries and Etta insisted on keeping a kosher home where she sang as she cooked, ironed, and boiled diapers for Freyde's baby brother.

Freyde was helpful as she handed her mother each clean diaper to hang on the clothesline. She had never been in trouble except for once when she grabbed her mother's favorite glass

Clockwise from above:
The Samovar; Vinegar
Rocker with Freyde and
Joy: Joy and Freyde play
on the sidewalk

bowl and galloped off. When Freyde tripped, the bowl broke into too many pieces to glue back together. Her Mother, Etta, cried out then as always, *"Ye gods and little fishes."* Although Asher loved his daughter, he spanked her anyway because in those days some parents spanked.

With tears in her eyes Freyde looked out her bedroom window and across the street where she saw a tiny girl with yellow hair and bangs on her forehead, surely a Dutch princess, sitting on her personal throne on the sidewalk in front of her house. A baby doll was tucked beside her in the bright red Adirondack chair that fit her perfectly. The little girl wore red sneakers to match the chair. In truth she always wore at least one red sneaker, though sometimes two, depending on how fast she'd been running.

The princess' name was Joy and at four years old she was about to score her first great victory. She put her hands on her hips that day and announced to the neighborhood boys that she no longer intended to play with them because now she had a girlfriend. Freyde was the beneficiary, though being only three, she needed guidance to cross safely to the other side of the street to begin the friendship that was to last a lifetime.

The little girls played chase every day, salted and nibbled tiny green apples, and discovered some bug that required attention. Soon enough though, they became students and trooped off down the hill, one after the other, to kindergarten and first grade. They were reading about the Bobbsey twins while Joy's mother, Buddy Rose, cooked and pulled batches of vinegar taffy for them. They'd carry a chunk of the sticky candy with them to Joy's bright and airy side porch and to their perches that were the wide arms of a sturdy wicker rocking chair. Its cratered seat supported a faded cushion for their feet.

That screened verandah with the old rocker was a perfect space to read, rock, and chew. Here was a still zone a world apart from the hectic pace at Freyde's house where she was sandwiched between two opinionated brothers and rarely experienced anything remotely resembling peace.

Joy's house remained a haven in those days because Buddy Rose never seemed angry even when the girls yanked her best clothes off closet hangers to play dress up, dabbed on her Evening in Paris, or picked out the hexagonal tiles under her upstairs bathroom sink. Buddy Rose never considered the girls malicious because theirs was a genuine belief they'd land in China.

Across the street in Freyde's house her mother, Etta, sang day in and day out. She sang all the words to "Me and My Shadow" for Freyde and Joy and called them the Gold Dust Twins even though they looked nothing alike. On Shabbos, Freyde was at her dining room table with hands scrubbed clean well before the streetlights came on. No Friday night passed without lighting the candles before a hearty meal of roasted chicken or brisket which Etta koshered herself once a month after the butcher delivered his order. Although Joy never ate Friday suppers with Freyde, she absorbed baruch atah adonai, the opening to many of the Hebrew prayers. Joy, too, could recite the Shema but spent Sunday mornings at a local church where she put a donation dime in the plate when it came around while Freyde, at Hebrew school, pressed her dime into a tri-fold booklet for a tree in Israel.

Sometimes together and sometimes apart, the little girls

grew taller and smarter. During elementary school and junior high Freyde collected Joy every morning for the walk to school. She learned patience as Buddy Rose insisted that Joy eat a good breakfast before she left the house: one fresh egg in the eggcup with toast points was good nourishment to hold her until lunchtime.

Once a week Joy and Freyde went to the library and occasionally sneaked into the grownups' section in search of contraband. When Etta saw Marjorie Morningstar lying on Freyde's bed, she realized that the girls were growing up. She'd recently given them permission to ride their bicycles the 20-miles roundtrip to Louisa May Alcott's house. Neither mother, however, was aware that the girls' shoes lay hidden in their baskets under movie magazines. It was the age of the hippie and these girls were oh so cool.

After wandering through the center entrance colonial Orchard House and listening for the ghosts of Amy, Jo, Beth, and Meg, Freyde and Joy rode on to Thoreau's Walden Pond where they heard about an interesting concept called "civil disobedience." It held little meaning for either Freyde, who was an obedient daughter, or for Joy, whose civil disobedience extended only as far as sassing her mother, Buddy Rose.

In short time the young ladies fell in love, and oddly enough, with the same man, Elvis Swivelhips Presley. On piano lesson day, they'd load up their movie magazines and piano music into their bookbags and ride the trolley, complaining the whole way about their teacher. Then they'd muddle their way sequentially through their lessons, stroll to the sandwich shop in the center of town to select the best dill pickle in the barrel, dig it out of the brine, purse their lips even before sampling it, and make their way up Mass Ave toward Farrington's record store. There they'd spend a dollar each for the latest Elvis release, leaving just enough change for carfare and a quarter pound of pistachios which were a dollar a pound. After lurching their way off the trolley near home, they'd wave to Sam, the dry goods man, who conversed during his summer vacations on a Saratoga Springs park bench with a Supreme Court Justice, for in those days anyone could be somebody and nobodies were sometimes somebodies.

Two days a week, Freyde studied Hebrew with the five other Jewish children in town. Along with her partners they watched out the window for the 5 o'clock train instead of paying attention to the rabbi and their translation of Genesis from Hebrew to English. The tiny class was impatient as it wondered how many different ways those words describing the first days of creation could be dissected. Admittedly, God's accomplishment was outstanding, but Freyde thought it was time to move on to Exodus.

In addition to studying her Hebrew vocabulary and practicing the piano, Freyde was also responsible for polishing her mother's samovar. It occupied the place of honor in her house where it rested on the mantle above the fireplace. Having been handed down to the oldest girl in each generation, it was now Etta's treasure. This particular samovar was short and stubby with but a few minor dents in its brassy shine to reflect its journey to America in the belly of steerage class. Nothing in its patina revealed the unsettling diaspora of its former owners who were running from pogroms and conscription to the land where the streets were paved in gold. The metaphorical gold of America was the opportunity to own a house in certain towns or certain sections of town and to send children to public school where they learned Christmas carols and could be angels in the pageant. And in America one's children and grandchildren could buy a pharmacy or go to law school. While Yiddish schools diminished in numbers in America, Yiddish remained but a secret language primarily for the old folks, including Freyde's bubbie and zayde, to foil the little pitchers with big ears.

Although the samovar now belonged to Etta, she'd never used it or even seen it used for heating water for tea. But Etta had loved the polishing as a girl and young married woman. She intuitively understood, perhaps from a vague memory of her own polishing days, that Freyde would only come to love the samovar if she cared for it herself. So Freyde began polishing at a young age since it was Etta's way of preparing Freyde for her turn as its keeper.

By the time Freyde and Joy were 14 and 15 the momentous occasions of their first kisses became talking points between them. It felt more like a slap than a kiss, one girl said, while the other insisted it was just plain weird. But they took those milestones in stride never mentioning their secrets to Etta or Buddy Rose as they graduated to <u>Gone With the Wind</u>. Joy learned then, from Buddy Rose, that her grandmother, Catherine, now deceased and but a shadow in their lives, despised the egocentric Scarlett O'Hara. This simple fact brought Catherine to life for Joy.

✺

Life continued in song with Etta singing "Sixteen Tons" and across the street Buddy Rose laughing as she woke and reawoke her sleepyhead girl in the mornings, boiling those three and a half minute eggs, escaping into her favorite magazines and driving the girls to Plum Cove in Annisquam.

The homes were happy houses for Joy and Freyde and the girls were changing quickly. Joy's Easy Bake oven was donated to the church rummage sale and her Buster Browns morphed into Capezios. Freyde's tin dollhouse disappeared into the attic and three starched petticoats took over her triangle of a closet. And Elvis, the love of their lives, was driven off by the twin demons of Latin and English. No time was left for The King after the piano, the samovar, the sock hops, the formals, and translations of Caesar, Cicero and Virgil. These girls were determined to avoid disappointing their Latin teacher, Miss Domina Rotunda, who demanded disclosure including a full and prompt confession if daily translations were not completed when one was called upon to recite in the daily cat and mouse game. "I am not prepared, Miss Rounds," was the preferred language to announce to her and the class that she was snared and about to be sacrificed. And then the dedicated Miss Rounds painstakingly notated a perfect zero beside the unlucky name in her grade book. Meanwhile, in a tribute to her personal style, which the girls described as similar to Dracula-on-the-prowl, Miss Rounds scrawled on the blackboard the dreadful words, Horribile Dictu and Horribile Visu and then embellished her letters with swirls and swoops as she drove in her shaming verbal stakes.

After the stress of the school year, the summer that Freyde turned 15 and Joy 16, began with promise. Joy had a new boyfriend and Freyde was learning to type at summer school, for

33

everyone in the 1950s knew that typing was a critical skill for a young woman. One sunny morning in late June with lilac in the air, Freyde's little brother charged down the hill to meet her after class. He was gasping as he shouted out that something bad, really bad, had happened to Joy's mother, Buddy Rose. The ambulance had taken her away, dead from a heart attack. It seemed impossible to Freyde that while she was typing a row of a–s–d–f's, Buddy Rose was dying, so the natural thing to do was to accuse her brother of being a spoiled-bratty-rotten liar which he remained for five minutes until Etta corroborated the awful truth.

Freyde raced up the stairs to her room and slammed the door behind her as if it were her brother's fault for delivering the news. She crumpled on the bed in misery and used up every tissue in her Kleenex box. Where was Joy? And, no, she would not come out of her room for supper, she screamed at her father. And where had Joy gone? And no one would ever sing again and the happy house on Ashland would be a morgue forever. And why wasn't Joy home? And they could both just forget vinegar taffy and Scarlett OHara, that hussy, and swimming in Plum Cove. Etta didn't drive so that was the end of the beach. Freyde stopped her silent rants every now and then to look out the window for Joy and finally understood that this was about Joy and about Buddy Rose because her own mother was alive downstairs in the kitchen and she could still jump rope, red hot pepper.

Freyde's mind wound itself in circles of confusion that day as the one most important question fixed itself in her mind. Who would make Joy's egg? Did her father even know how to make an egg, a three-and-a-half -minute egg? Since Death was hideous and unthinkable, the obsessive question of the egg became strangely central as it wedged itself in Freyde's mind. Get it wrong and the egg would be either a runny inedible mess or a dried out lump. Get it just right and with a spoon Joy could dig it out of the shell from her eggcup. And then maybe it wouldn't matter so much if Buddy Rose wasn't around. That was Freyde's mixed up reasoning on that gorgeous summer day.

◖◉

The rest of the summer passed in the warmest of hazes, and Joy put one foot in front of the other to complete her senior year of high school. No one could ever know what it was like for her to walk into that empty foyer after school without Buddy Rose there to greet her. The house was now devoid of genuine pleasure because Buddy Rose with her high rouged cheekbones wasn't there to laugh, cook, and guide Joy around the potholes that opened out of nowhere. While her father made eggnog for Joy, life was never the same for either of them. Buddy Rose, they discovered, had been the light and the soul of their home. She was the one who picked up fallen apples, cleaned out the gravel cuts on Joy's knees, located the missing sneaker, and pulled the taffy.

Joy ditched school at least 30 days her senior year and attached herself to "American Bandstand" on television as she and Freyde strolled and ponied in her living room. And when the high school guidance counselor picked out a Seven Sister's college for her, it seemed a perfect strategy to get Joy back in the groove. She was smart, socially skilled and would surely rule the roost on campus.

❦

College life proved to be a new beginning and Joy loved her new batch of friends. Her letters to Freyde who was still stuck in high school were enthusiastic, and that's how Freyde landed at the same college the next year in a dormitory directly across the quadrangle from Joy's. But on one sweltering night during spring finals, with all the windows of the quad dormitories open to the damp night air, Joy's terrible loss caught up with her. Freyde heard a raw and extended scream as it pierced the silence from the direction of Joy's dorm and she knew as if she were Buddy Rose that this was her Joy, unglued Joy, unhinged Joy, frantic Joy. She raced down four flights of stairs and around toward the streak that was her best friend since she was three and just in time to intercept her on her sprint to nowhere.

❦

After a yearlong break when Joy became a speedy typist, she returned to college where she and Freyde, roommates finally, graduated together. A month later with no lightning bolts flashing, no celestial angels hovering, and no words written in the wind, Joy married her longtime boyfriend, Robert. Slowly and with dedication to each other they created another happy house, their own happy house, very much like the one Joy knew on Ashland Street.

Over the years Joy gave birth to four children. She baked, laughed, pulled vinegar taffy and invoked the memory of Buddy Rose every step of the way. She hosted open houses and birthday parties, and she wrote detailed 20-page letters to Freyde, all the while missing her beloved mother but carrying on in the best Buddy Rose tradition.

C

Fast forward to the spring of 1971.

Freyde was watching Sesame Street in New Orleans with her two-year-old daughter and delighted by the excellent reception from her rabbit-eared television when she received a long distance call from Joy. It was a call during daylight hours and that meant it was something serious. Joy's voice was shaky with the kind of excitement one might expect if a man had taken a walk on the

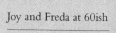

Joy and Freda at 60ish

moon, which, by the way, had just happened. Joy blurted out the news, the stunning news, that a family secret had been revealed.

Joy's Grandmother, Catherine, who despised Scarlet O'Hara, was Jewish. That made Buddy Rose Jewish if she'd chosen to claim her heritage. And what did that mean for Joy? At the very least, she and Freyde decided, as they laughed and cried, it meant that they shared yet one more bond, a sheltering chuppah of spirit that had embraced them during all of those growing up years. The graciousness with which Buddy Rose lived was imbued with Jewish mitzvah, that which she'd learned from her mother Catherine and, remarkably, all with shabbos candles in her heart though not on the table.

Freyde couldn't wait to tell her mother the secret of Buddy Rose's family.

"Why?" Freyde asked her mother, "Why did Catherine refuse to live as a Jew?"

"It's not ours to know or to judge," Etta said, invoking the wisdom of her grandfather, Rabbi Baruch Cohen. "Remember, Freyde," she spoke in a voice only a little above a whisper, "it's not always easy to be a Jew. There were times when it was very dangerous." No doubt Etta was thinking of her own family from Lithuania, shot to death in the Holocaust. Etta continued, "We didn't walk in Catherine's or Buddy Rose's shoes. We must remember that Catherine's gifts to Buddy Rose and Buddy Rose's gifts to Joy are what matter. Those gifts were like God's gifts to Moses who cared for the Commandments, brought them down the mountain, and passed them along to us for generation upon generation."

Freyde couldn't sleep that night as she imagined the dilemma Catherine faced when she let go of the label while keeping the commitment of creating happiness. She'd carefully molded Buddy Rose's world, imprinting for her how to duplicate a joyous haven for her own golden girl.

❦

The girls, Freyde and Joy, are still the best of friends. They learned from their mothers who learned from theirs. They believe that by now their gifts are embedded into genetic code for the generations. Freyde is hopeful that she has inherited and passed along far more than a recessive gene for red-hair and a tendency toward compulsive research, and Joy feels certain she has inherited from Catherine, by way of Buddy Rose, an inextinguishable spirit of honor, respect and, always…joy.

Joy is grandmother to a small pack of children for whom she boils those three-and-a-half-minute eggs. You could say she's a Bubbie to those children just as her friend, Freyde, is Bubbie to her pack of six grandchildren, little acorns all, the oldest of whom is already polishing the samovar and making the past a part of her future.

Every year when Freyde and Joy light the yahrzeit candles for Etta who died at age 93 and for Buddy Rose who died at age 55, they remember their mothers and recall the blessed tradition of the happy house.

Shiva Candle Skeptic

Mother died at age 93 and although I don't like to mention this, I was prepared to feel, to believe, and to accept that the weight of sadness would be lifted. I'd bought into the conventional wisdom that encourages one to feel "relief" once a person's suffering is finally over. I believed we should now put all our loved one's misery, and our own, behind us. It was something like the whole "closure" lie.

Okay, I told myself. Mother is buried now and the handful of dirt straight from Israel was sprinkled into her grave. I've tossed a shovelful of dirt into the open grave on top of her casket to bring home to me the awful reality that it's finished and she's left us. Casket and sad case closed. I would pack my suitcase, write the checks for the bereavement luncheon, clean up from shiva, hop on the airplane and head home to write my thank-you's to all our helpful and compassionate friends and family.

But the case was not closed at all and the peace I'd hoped for did not settle over me. I couldn't sleep while snippets from

Mother's last two months were replaying nonstop in my mind like the Elvis records from my childhood. First, I was repeating verbatim clips of my conversations with her before she was no longer able to speak with me, my brothers, or her caregivers. And these morphed into conversations with myself in which I second-guessed every decision we made. I was tormented by recollections and visions of my dear mother. Rather than getting dimmer, these thoughts became more substantive. I was off balance, distracted, and wondering if I could have contracted a mild case of post-traumatic stress syndrome. Death might be a normal part of the life cycle, but Mother's passing had slammed me.

My husband was taking the brunt of it as I kept talking "at" him. I spoke in circles about what I could have or should have done and questioned endlessly why I hadn't done it this way or that way in order to mitigate the distress of her last months. I was not letting go of anything and even if no blame existed, I blamed myself anyway. This was more than simple Jewish guilt. I was perseverating and I doubt I was pleasant to be around.

Untouched on my kitchen counter was a small shopping bag from the funeral chapel and after a few days at home, I dared peek inside. The contents included a simple leatherette binder with the sign-in log of funeral attendees, the list of future yahrzeit dates, the death certificates which I could not bear to look at with Mother's cause of death and the time that Sunday she left us. Nowhere on that certificate was it noted that the afternoon was exceptionally brilliant with the afternoon sun pouring into her twelfth floor windows to warm her cold body.

And, finally, the funeral bag contained a tall shiva candle

in a glass with its eternal light printed on the front. I hadn't lit it during the shiva in the hotel suite because I didn't know the correct prayer, I had no matches, and I admit to thinking it seemed a little hocus pocus.

I should reveal here and now my personal cop-out: that I take pride in being "culturally Jewish" and can cook up fabulous blintzes and latkes, but I've forgotten most of my Hebrew from six dedicated years of Hebrew school while my friends were tap dancing. Lame excuses, perhaps, but then wasn't the shiva candle some sort of atavistic relic like the custom of burying a fleishik spoon in the dirt if it accidentally encountered ice cream?

I'd seen a squat version of that yahrzeit relic in my Bubbie's house 60 years ago and can still hear her as she rocked and complained beside the flame, "Shayna madelah...why don't you cut your bangs?"

I glanced into the bag at my unlighted and unremarkable shiva candle several times before determining it would be as sacreligious to throw it in the junk as to bury Mother without reciting the prayers for the dead. How could it hurt to light the candle in honor of my orthodox mother who kept paper plates available in case a goyische friend should visit the house bearing pepperoni pizza. The shiva candle would serve as a backup honor secondary only to my making certain the chevra kadisha was involved in preparing Mother's body with respect, washing her and dressing her in fresh white muslin. Burning the candle was the least I could do.

As I lit the candle, minus a prayer, I recalled how I honored Mother in her lifetime with visits, telephone calls, birthday parties and gifts, how I slaved over blintzes for her just a few months ago, wearing my decrepit running shoes to keep myself from collapsing from the tedium of my efforts at the stove, one crepe at a time. But to me, being a generation more enlightened than Mother and just a half step ahead of the feminists who burned their bras, honoring Mother meant I was resolute as I brushed off her comment, whispered at me when she was only 90, that I should just do a graveside burial so as not to interfere with anyone's schedule. It was typical of Mother who was always on someone else's journey in spite of being an attorney by the age of 21. She would forget how deserving she was as a dedicated mom and an always-available support staffer. As far as I was concerned, Mother was going to be subjected to that special funeral even if it was 20 degrees below zero. And wouldn't Mother have been tickled pink (her words, not mine) that God or our good fortune blew a record setting warm day into Boston on December 3, 2009, the day she was laid to rest, honored by her family and friends.

I trimmed the wick and lit the shiva candle to honor Mother, all the while believing the gesture was completely altruistic. Every time I walked into and out of the kitchen, passing by the shiva candle, my conversations with myself began anew, sometimes repetitive and sometimes lighting up new and cursed memories. Why hadn't I remembered how effective the Tylenol was and why hadn't I searched more drugstores to find the adult liquid form? Why exactly had my brothers and I decided against getting her knee X-rayed after she fell? Why, in God's name, hadn't we left her in peace to sleep? She hated noise, so why were her caregivers so loud in her ear? I watched it go on and must have been numb to let that continue. Did we really think Mother could recover without functioning heart valves? How could we have been in such denial?

The loving caregivers were preparing food three ways and yelling in her ear to wake up and taste. Fulfilling their mission to perfection, they blended and chopped and fed her with straws and teaspoons to nourish her. They were keeping her alive with textbook care.

I berated myself every time I passed the shiva candle. But in silent dialogue I answered myself with my best and most robust arguments. "How do you know she wouldn't recover with good nutrition? You are not God." "But," I would answer myself, "she clearly wanted to sleep. She would not and could not open her eyes." Then, "Even if she could open her eyes, she could not see me or recognize me." And, "What makes you so sure she did not know you were there?" I answered myself. Layered over my constant dialogue, like Hollywood voiceovers, were Mother's thin, kittenlike screams as the caregivers moved her 90-pound body with its torn knee. Before long I would walk past the candle to another room, shutting down for a small moment my internal voice, in order to take care of my daily life.

Time after time that first week after she died I self-talked myself through the pain of the last few months. The candle burned steadily and reminded me that Mother was gone, but as I went out of sight of the candle, my tormented thoughts miraculously left me alone. The sorrowful thoughts restarted as I saw the shiva candle and then were tucked away as I walked past it and out of sight.

Remarkable is the perfect word to describe this talisman, my hocus pocus shiva candle, that triggered the processing to the conclusion, dare I say death, of my troubling thoughts. I walked through those unsettling dialogues with the unremarkable candle and now believe those seventeen generations of rabbis from whom I'm descended knew what they were doing. They surely recognized the therapeutic aspect of this phenomenon, for I believe that's just what it was. But even if no scientific analysis exists of how a shiva candle works to comfort a mourner, I can testify that once I blew it out after the weeklong burn, I had completed my metaphorical self-flagellation and began to remember the real mother who jumped rope with me, arrived on my doorstep with joy to help out when my babies were born, and reminded me it was unbecoming to hold a grudge.

Perhaps all's well that ends well. Mother always quoted a little Shakespeare. For sure, all the world's a stage and Mother will be tickled pink (her words, not mine) to see from above at center stage that her shiva candle worked its magic.

The Blintz As Metaphor

My kitchen and I had mostly parted ways when our younger child was sixteen. While cooking on occasions such as Thanksgiving, Christmas, and Passover was still a pleasure, the daily drudgery of chopping salads, trimming meat and making marinades had become a chore. We did continue to enjoy our container picnics on the beach, corned beef and cabbage dinners on St. Patrick's Day, and a New Orleans style red beans and rice on New Years Day. And if we scored fresh Gulf shrimp, I used my butter spattered <u>River Road Cookbook</u> and dug out my hand-crafted bibs and a roll of paper towels to mop up butter drippings. While we didn't have the benefit of statins to keep our artery plaques from rupturing, we were protected from fear by ignorance. We counted calories in and calories out.

So, my cooking became limited to occasion cooking. When the occasion was festive, I could prepare my Father Sarducci cheesecake. For my mother's visits, I baked sour cream softies and pineapple yogurt cake. For our son's birthdays, I whipped up

Rochel Varnick Neipris and A.T. Neipris; below, Cousin Rochel's blintzes

chocolate mousse from scratch, and for my husband, his mother's tapioca. For my father's pleasure I would grit my teeth and stink up the house with a giant pot of stuffed cabbage, the kind that has to cook with sour salts for at least 24 hours. My father doctored it up when he sprinkled in the brown sugar that would bring the cabbage rolls to perfection. My Russian grandparents would have been proud had they tasted this finely tuned stuffed cabbage. Even the raisins were plump with flavor.

But my tour de force was the cheese blintz. These always came out delicate and delicious, reminding me of days gone by, for I was a small child when I learned to love them. I confess my motivation was hardly pure, driven as it was by the rewards of praise from others, especially my hypercritical father. Ultimately, the process of making and completing the batches of blintzes became as symbolic as the chuppa at a Jewish wedding for the end result united the family in the midst of political battles such as the wisdom of engaging in the Viet Nam war or using bussing

47

to speed up integration. The blintz transcended all political and personal differences.

◈

As any artist knows, preparation is key. First, I locate pressed farmers cheese and stare at it in my refrigerator until the expiration date reads the next day and there's no turning back. I change into my blintz-making outfit that consists of running shoes, a full apron, a thin, comfortable jersey and loose fitting pants. The telephone answer machine is turned on to intercept all distracting phone calls; the wooden slammer board covered with a damp dish towel is set out on the counter; the butter sticks are turned out onto a curved saucer; the cookie sheets are buttered; hand towels are available and within reach. As soon as I set my iPod to Glenn Gould playing Bach's "Goldberg Variations," I begin cracking open the dozen eggs for the crepe batter. I'm off and running.

The batter for the first several blintzes is always lumpy, then too thick. I add a quarter cup of water until it reaches a consistency for the crepe to hold together but remains thin and pliable. Meanwhile, it takes a while for the crepe pan to reach the correct temperature. Too hot and the crepe burns quickly or too cool and each crepe takes more than a minute to cook. When factoring in buttering time between each skin, defective crepes, split, puny or overly thick crepes from the early batch, production time runs at least 60 minutes for only 30 crepes.

I swish the batter around the bottom of the pan, making certain it's cooked through before I bang it out onto the damp towel. That's the drill. But, if the crepe is stubborn or the pan gets too hot, I must gently peel it off the pan by hand.

Each part of the process was, is, and will always be mindless, while the ironic paradox remains. The final product is splendid. I pour, swish, and thump out the crepes one at a time onto the growing pile of finished crepes as I hear Glenn Gould humming along with his piano. (Part of the process is to wonder how Glenn could hum a Goldberg Variation.)

As I work I recall my father's unintentionally cruel statement. "My mother could make four at once in her giant cast iron skillet." I envisioned my Bubbie, like a short order cook, working four burners at a time in her Russian shtetl. Maybe instead of finely ornamented Baroque melodies to listen to, she had some clucking chickens underfoot.

As I hover over my stove, my mind has time to wander. One huge skillet could explain my Bubbie's oversized wrist and the gold bracelet that now belongs to me. When would she have had an occasion to wear such a heavy mesh bracelet? In her village of dusty streets, riding in a droshky behind a driver with a whip? While I'd never know the answer, I was certain that the family she created enjoyed her blintzes for they spoke of love and plenty and always transcended the mundane.

The plenty part, of course, was a lie. Poverty in my father's family was a fact, and my Uncle Alec, my Bubbie's firstborn, was undernourished and thin. In her new home in America, Bubbie would walk to the playground, called Ferry Way Green in Malden, Massachusetts, to plump up Alec with a half pint of cream. When you couldn't speak English in America AND you were small for your age, bullying was apt to be a problem. It was a moral imperative to grow Alec into a stronger kid. My own father, Usher, spoke only Yiddish until first grade when he learned English and his name then became Oscar.

By the time I was a bride and had my own kitchen, my Bubbie was too sick to teach me the art of the blintz, but I got lucky one winter. A real kitchen goddess, my Cousin Rochel Neipris, a first cousin once removed to my grandfather, Alter, came to New Orleans where we lived in order to visit her brother from South Africa. She'd loved me ever since she and her husband, A.T., took me to their house to care for me while my mother was hospitalized for several months. I was an infant and responded to their love originally lavished on their sons who were now married and on their own. Rochel had welcomed all sorts of immigrant relatives into her home and infant Freda was just one more transient guest.

Twenty-five years later Rochel dedicated three blessed days and nights to me in New Orleans and that's when I learned to make blintzes. We began my lessons with a simple baked flounder, challah and onion rolls, and we ended with…The Blintz. My rounded, blue-eyed, outspoken cousin with a case of serious glaucoma was at least 80 years old by then but had the stamina necessary to pass along her tried and true way to show love and respect.

I drop the spoonful of egg, sugar, and cheese filling toward one end of the round crepe that I tuck up from the edges and roll over and lay on its seam onto the buttered cookie sheet. My father will love these. My mother will be proud. She'll tell me again that her own mother was dead by the time she'd turned 40 years old. As for her own deficit in the blintz department, she'll remind me that there was no time to learn such an art with all those diapers to boil and hang out to dry? Who had time what with whooping cough and a preemie, Mother would ask.

I put the tray of blintzes in the freezer for 40 minutes and then carefully deposit them into a plastic bag to finish freezing until it's time to fry them up.

✺

Time went by and my father died. I helped turn off his respirator and recall the rotten grimace of his last moment. To forget that minute, I force myself to remember all that I did for his love. "Where can you get a blintz like this?" he'd say. "These would cost two dollars each...*if* you could even find them!"

So, then I made my blintzes for Mother until she could no longer ingest a speck of sodium. And after Mother, who was so proud, died at 93, I made the blintzes for Eli, Rochel's son, now a very old man of 97 who is reminded of his mother in a bittersweet way whenever he eats my blintzes that are her blintzes.

I part with each blintz as if it's gold, and before I serve blintzes to a guest, I do a mental assessment during which I attempt to measure his or her deservedness and appreciation for the act of loving kindness that's built into each blintz.

Because I want to pass along the art of the blintz to the next generation, I'm committed to a serious mission that I believe is an obligation. I've scheduled a Blintz clinic in my kitchen at which time I will hand the torch to my children and grandchildren. I dare wait no longer. Who knows what cruel act of fate could intervene to derail my careful plan?

Cousin Rochel's blintzes and blintz techniques may seem standard, but miraculously her recipe never fails to neutralize or deflect tension, frustration, hurt and fear. Unlike chicken soup that is a staple, a blintz, a Cousin Rochel blintz in particular, includes the lagniappe of love. Like any other treasured heirloom, her blintz, now my blintz, has meaning. My granddaughters and Rochel's granddaughter and great grandsons, too, will soon own a piece of family history, an art learned in Lithuania in another century.

A Golden Box of Bones

Sister Mariette Caron Paquin may have seen the torrential rain as a sign from God. Or perhaps she wondered if God Herself summoned the rain to catapult us from Rue Charlevoix in Quebec City into the hospital-museum through the only unlocked door we could find. Our clothes were soaked as we stumbled into the Hotel-Dieu de Quebec where the St. Augustine nuns had labored for centuries caring for orphans, the sick and the needy. Without a human being in sight, this cellar provided us tranquil shelter in stark contrast to the driving outdoor rainstorm.

No signs and no entrance fees provided clues about where we'd landed, so we wandered through the unguarded cave of the basement with its original stone foundation from 1695. Newer artifacts from more recent centuries were scattered here and there obviously with the confidence that thieves would never consider pilfering the relics.

When a woman appeared from a tiny side office to greet us as guests and not trespassers, we were relieved. Sister Mariette

Caron Paquin wore sensible shoes and the clothing of a modern day sister. She ushered us ever so gently into a bright and modern little chapel. We were God's Chosen People that day and Sister Mariette treated us with honor.

A small gilded box lit up the room and was the clear focal point in the tiny chapel with its red carpet. The box was a reliquary, Sister Mariette explained. It held the bones of Sister Marie Catherine who was among the earliest settlers of Quebec and was said to be the co-founder of the Catholic Church in Canada. My first thought was that those old bones were surely a pile of dust after almost 350 years. I had empirical evidence of this transition from bone to dust after collecting our son's baby teeth from the tooth fairy and saving them in a matchbox. When I parted with those teeth 25 years later, they'd crumbled within the tiny box as nondescript dust along with my nostalgia for the lost days of his babyhood.

Another thought popped into my skeptical mind as I stared at the golden box. Was it possible or likely that there were no bones inside? Snake oil and Carter's Little Liver Pills. Impossible, I told myself, that The Church would perpetrate a hoax around such an important person on route to sainthood. I shook off the notion of that particular heresy and accepted that some bones were inside. Okay then, would DNA verify their legitimacy as belonging to Sister Marie Catherine? I'd heard of too many hoaxes lately around shadows and Rorschach-type stains. My mind was spiraling into negativity and disbelief. My evidenced-based take on life was depriving me of a charming moment in time and I knew it.

Clockwise from above:
Sister Marie Catherine;
Sister Marie Catherine's
reliquary; turntable receptacle
for accepting abandoned
babies

Sister Mariette, speaking to us from beside the reliquary, became more animated as she spoke of the complexities of Sister Marie Catherine's life. Her eyes were bright with admiration and I was thoroughly engaged by her story, as well as the love she projected for Sister Marie Catherine. She leaned toward me with a Madonna tilt to her head and supplicant hands as she described the life of this sad and inspired child.

Marie Catherine was only 12 years old when she became a postulant and took the habit of the Augustinian Hospitaller Sisters of the Mercy of Jesus. She was 16 when she left her grandmother's home in Normandy, France to sail to Quebec. The three-month crossing nearly killed her and she claimed to have been attacked by dragons. When she finally landed, she was taken to the hospital where she knocked at the same door through which we'd entered. While we barged through seeking shelter, Sister Marie Catherine had arrived to offer herself to God for service on Earth.

⟨⟨☉

I listen carefully to the story but am thinking about dragons and wonder if Sister Marie Catherine was suffering hallucinations from high fevers. Sister Mariette refocuses my interest in the story as she describes the fierce Indian natives and how Sister Marie Catherine learns their language in order to teach catechism to them. People everywhere love her good sense and hard work. Before long, Sister's mentor, Father de Brebeuf, is martyred (murdered) by the Iroquois, and he appears frequently in visions to Sister Marie Catherine. (I diagnose her with a suspected case of post-traumatic stress disorder.) But Sister Marie Catherine is tormented and tempted, feeling impure and ashamed that she's yearning for France. (Surely an overdeveloped conscience and spirit of perfectionism.) She feels sinful and that's tough to handle, especially for a Sister. So, Sister Marie Catherine fasts, sleeps on a hard bed and prays extra hard. And to gain mastery over her homesickness, she makes a perpetual vow never to leave Canada; yet, she's plagued with disquieting visions. She sees purgatory and people who are dead or sainted. (I wonder if she's working with mercury or any other chemicals at the hospital.) She announces deaths in France before the news has reached Quebec. And interspersed among her prayers and her ministering to the orphans, the sick and the needy is the added curse of alcohol, "firewater plague," among the unruly Native Americans. Meanwhile God permits devils to inhabit her body so they will not pester others. She is badly beaten by those same devils who then become an obsession. The young Sister Marie Catherine is dead by age 36. The year is 1668.

Our dedicated guide leads us even closer to the golden box itself and says, "Pope John Paul II, you know, beatified Blessed Sister Marie Catherine on Easter Sunday, April 23, 1989." Sister Mariette is serenity personified as she speaks English to us in a quiet voice with a French accent.

I want to whoop and cheer knowing how much Sister Marie Catherine deserves this honor from The Church. We're in the spiritual presence of a great woman and I'm beginning to feel an aura from the Blessed Sister Marie Catherine. Or am I sensing the gentle spirit of Sister Mariette infiltrating the space?

"We need just one more miracle," she tells us. I know she

needs our help and it seems almost like a plea. "Would you like to make a novena? Please?"

I'm Jewish is the only response I can think of although I really want to give her that miracle to elevate the Blessed Marie Catherine to sainthood. Sister Mariette needs an evidence based, real live miracle and she has a belief that I am serious, though perhaps not a believer. She thinks I can help her produce it.

She presses into my hand a two-inch-by-four-inch paper envelope with a novena card inside and makes me promise to let her know when my prayers are answered. Not wanting to ruin anyone's chances for success, I confess that I'm not experienced in prayer although I know it's not exactly the right place to launch into an explanation that I'm more of a cultural Jew who makes enviable blintzes. So I ask her for guidance with the novena.

⟨⟨⊙

I believe Sister Mariette understood that her detailed story of Sister Marie Catherine, a woman from a different century who knew only giving, caring and love of God, would say something profound to me. She may have sized up my need for a spiritual message by the intensity of my listening. Or, maybe Sister Mariette simply thought she was intervening in a chaotic life and could spur me toward meaningful prayer that would open my eyes. The simple answer may be that she was content to provide respite while the rain came down. But I think she had a sixth sense that I was really hearing her story. Our connection for our short moments together was as organic as any I'd ever experienced.

Since that meeting with Sister Mariette I've tried to make

sense of my powerful reaction to the visit with her and her beatified Sister Marie-Catherine. I've come to believe that I've let go some excitement as well as a piece of my younger and more enthusiastic self when I programmed myself to demand proof and evidence for everything in my life. While I'd never want to dial back the scientific progress of our generation, I'm left with the uncertainty of how to allow ambiguity into my world. Lately, I'm not compelled to look for the strings or wires behind the curtain at Disney World. I can enjoy seeing a body rise up from her coffin and hover while I clap along with the rest of the magic show audience.

Faith, hope and charity? It's easy to be good at charity but most of us have seen too much to be good at hope. Faith, the way Mariette sees it, is a miracle to be arriving soon. When it appears, I will not dismiss it as a coincidence. The same door to the hospital opened for us as it did for Sister Marie Catherine. She made her way into history with her grace and prayer, and through her medium, Sister Mariette, she touched two impatient Americans who'd forgotten that enchantment still exists in this world.

Shattered

It was not a dark and stormy night but a bright and early spring morning when I was reminded that few things in this world remain static. My husband and I were jolted awake by a loud whack in another part of the house. At first we thought a cookie sheet had fallen onto the tile floor of the pantry but it wasn't so much a crash as a powerful boom. Could the ceiling fan have landed on the dining room table?

I staggered out of bed with a pounding heart and noticed our aqua stretch glass bowl lying in several pieces on the library table in the foyer where it had lived comfortably for years. I was puzzled. We live without cats, children, or opera singers; we have no temperature extremes, earthquakes, or construction dynamiting.

Our nearly 100-year-old, perfect bowl had survived transport from the Central Valley of California where I bought it 25 years earlier to Corona del Mar, California and then to Upstate New York. Recent temperatures had fluctuated between 60 and 70 degrees and there was no direct sunlight on the bowl. Keys were never dropped carelessly, or at all, into that bowl. And I'd erased

Heraclitus[1] from memory by the time I went on summer break after freshman year in college. From my perspective all conditions seemed perfect for serenity in our home at the time of the spontaneous shattering.

After the crash I ran to check on the condition of my grandmother Molly's stretch glass bowl, but it remained quiescent on a sofa table in the living room. Then I grabbed our camera to document this event that I hoped wasn't a precursor to a large earthquake or other such cataclysm. Had my great grandfather, Rabbi Baruch Cohen, buried long ago in Tel Aviv in Trumpeldor Street Cemetery, sent a malicious dybbuk to warn me of something about to happen? Had he finally gotten around to being upset that I'd interrupted a stellar lineage of 17 generations of rabbis to marry a WASP with a 3rd after his name?

For an instant I anthropomorphized that the bowl was angry because I'd recently brought home a stack of new Peggy Karr glass. Fearing a loss of status if I were to replace it with a piece of that newfangled art glass, it may have preferred, in a histrionic fit of self-pity, to self-destruct rather than be demoted to a dark cabinet or, god forbid, banished to our outdoor storage unit, a purgatory for broken ginger jar lamps and pictures.

[1]Heraclitus believed that change is the fundamental essence of the universe, as suggested by his famous statement, "No man ever steps in the same river twice."

⟨@

After fires, tornadoes, hurricanes, and floods have destroyed all property including family photos, collections and personal treasures, grateful victims conclude that, thanks to God, they've at least survived. I've often empathized for a moment with their terrible losses but am soon tugged back to my reality and get on with life among my old books and heirlooms. Maybe I straighten a photo on my Dead Wall, vacuum my Oriental rugs, or clean a closet to decide if this is finally the year to purge my letters from 50 years ago. Maybe I re-read some of those I wrote to my parents during my college years and with revisionist nostalgia recapture an exciting youth. Or, maybe I tear apart my photo albums that were once in perfect chronological order to redistribute to grown children, old friends, and good homes before they're trashed.

My stuff has brought me comfort throughout my lifetime. As shallow as that seems, it's an indisputable fact that I cherish important bits and pieces of my life—Aunt Sarah's wedding present afghan, my recipe box filled with other people's favorites which are now my favorites, my grandmother's samovar, the candy scale from my father's drugstore, and my great Uncle Max's black iron date stamps from his clothing store, now bookends. These and other tangibles mark my place in history and keep me from floating untethered in space. Because of them, I'm not "no one." I am the child, the girl, the young woman, and the old lady who is anchored to a family or a place or a time.

While I understand that all my stuff can be instantly demolished in an explosion or a natural disaster, and the cognitively capable me is aware of the ephemeral nature of my treasured belongings, those thoughts are themselves fleeting. I desperately want to continue leaning on the notion of the dependability of the things around me, such as the painting given to me on the occasion of my 50th birthday and entitled "Sunrise For Freda." That painting reminds me of the relative nature of feeling old and discourages the impatient me from surfacing.

Imbued with metaphor is my brass table lugged by my great auntie on board a ship from Palestine all the way to New York in 1934. It's engraved with Hebrew letters, שלך הפה בגג להיאחז יכול שלך הלשון ירושלים את שוכח אני אם whose translation is, "If I forget you, Jerusalem, may my tongue cling to the roof of my mouth." And then there's my grand piano that was bought with my inheritance from my Grandpa Alter, one of only two members of his family who wasn't shot to death in his beloved Lithuania during the Holocaust. This was the same grandpa who worked in the Chelsea Naval Yard and lived at the YMCA. When I polish that piano it sings to me of the American Dream that has the potential to come true. One artifact after another in my home triggers memories and reminders that I've lived a rich and blessed life.

But the shattering of my bowl shook me out of complacency.

I alerted my friends and family to the bizarre explosion of my old glass bowl. I hoped one of them might have an explanation.

Some were doubters:

"Ummm…sounds like a mystery to me!" Sybil mulls it over.

"I'm very glad your bowl broke and that you didn't just imagine it." Alfred, always the skeptic, implying mental illness?

"Fascinating." Mary loves a good mystery, especially when something is lost.

Then came the Inspector Clouseau comment from one of my friends:

"Good morning Freda, I am wondering if there was a barometric change outside that could have affected pressure in your house. Also, is it at all possible there's a hairline crack you might not have seen? But still there had to be some reason logically for it to break. I am going to investigate further. Interesting." Alma.

And then people commented who clearly believe they have more important things to worry about. *"Freda, Bad Vibrations. I recommend the Beach Boys song as a consolation."* Brother #1.

"Did Brother #1 send you Good Vibrations? I think your other two brothers are pretty creative." Brother #3.

"I'm afraid the correct explanation is that 'Shit Happens.'" No attribution.

And then our engineer son, suddenly a glass expert forever erring on the side of complicating matters: *"If a truck were to rumble by with just the right frequency, it conceivably might cause this type of catastrophic failure. The thickness of the base debunks the 'gravity' phenomenon that is another common cause of unexplained glass breakage in untempered antique glassware."* Daniel.

Or this.referencing Gilbert and Sullivan's HMS Pinafore, *"T'was the cat!"* It's the only good explanation. Brother #3 again.

Other people enjoyed being creative at my expense, of course: *"Since I know you would never own a cat because you're allergic, I dismiss Alfred's explanation. I also dismiss the idea of a ghost. Since the glass is an inanimate object without the possibility of feeling, I rule out jealousy. So what do we have left? Spontaneous combustion or as Cole Porter said, 'It is just one of those things.'"* Joyce.

Suddenly Alma was talking to a stranger, Joyce, drawn together by this mysterious event: *"What cat? Does she have a cat? I did not think so. Could have been the truck and perhaps a small unseen crack. I mean a microscopic one. It just might have done it in. You know a hand blown piece also could have had a thinner area that you might not see."* Alma Again.

Who was talking to whom? Even I was confused by now.

"I did not think she had a cat.... I'm still thinking the truck might have sent out vibrations that possibly caused or enabled a hairline crack to happen.... It then might have split with a slight temperature change." Anonymous.

I wish I'd never asked for help. It was a cluster of unhelpful confusion: *Had I mentioned a truck? No cat...no truck...no hairline fracture. Then, to add insult to injury Google was spying and lo... Steuben was marketing its wares as though a piece of Steuben could replace this old exploding piece of stretch glass. How totally spooky!* Me.

And, finally, one humble message arrived that defined a moral imperative for me along with a serious caveat: *"With regard to your self-destructing bowl, I have no guesses. To be on the safe side, however, you should make an effort to speak kindly to all the rest of your breakables."* Helen.

Exhausted by the unending speculation, I sent an email to the experts at Corning Museum of Glass, though not expecting a prompt response. I worried they'd consider me one of those loons who exists only to gather attention for a personal moment of fame.

To my great delight, Mr. David Whitehouse from Corning wrote:

Dear Freda,

Many thanks for your email. I suspect the cause of the problem goes all the way back to when the bowl was made. Glass that has been worked while it was hot needs to be annealed. Bringing it down from the working temperature to room temperature must be done gradually at a carefully controlled rate. If the glass cools too quickly, it will be highly strained by the time it reaches room temperature. Indeed, it may self-destruct before the cooling process is complete. On the other hand, it may survive for days, weeks, or even years before the strain causes it to break. (A few years ago, I examined a medieval beaker with polarizing filters and found that it had survived for 800 years despite being strained almost to breaking point.) I wonder: was your bowl in a spot that received direct sunlight during the day? If so, it is just possible that it heated up during the day and cooled down at night, and this eventually caused it to explode. I heard of a 100-year-old vase by the great French glassmaker Emile Galle that seems to have self-destructed for just such a reason.

Sincerely,

David Whitehouse

Mr. Whitehouse has now provided an answer though no reassurance that my other treasures will not self–destruct. At least I'm convinced this event was not caused by provocation on my part. Its demise was built into the bowl from the beginning like a poltergeist waiting to get out and get even.

As I deconstruct this incident, I notice that each of us processes information in a personal way that's congruent with his or her style. While the cautious Sybil doesn't have enough information to make a judgment, Alfred suggests that I may be unbalanced, and Joyce goes with the flow while she hums an appropriate Cole Porter song. Alma earnestly believes there's an explanation to be found and is willing to put in some time, and Helen teases me. Or is she suggesting that my breakables don't respect me and I'm involved in a lopsided love–hate relationship?

I, myself, hunt for meaning under every stone and view the occurrence either as mystical or as housing a moral metaphor. The literal wake-up call, the Big Bang as it were, has reminded me that not only is life fleeting but that the ending of all things often comes out of nowhere and when you're least expecting it. Magic is in the air and grabs my attention.

It's impossible to predict the demise either of human life or the inanimate objects we treasure. So, as Helen has suggested, we must make an effort to speak more kindly to the things and, by extension, the people we love. While I'm attempting to practice kindness and patience, I'm editing my worldview to accept that there may be a continuing process here that conforms to a Heraclitian rule of nature. I understand that I can no longer trust my belongings to be still and allow themselves to be dusted, shined, polished or even regarded with pleasure.

If there is a law of change and exchange at work, I'll accept that. Still, I'm lucky I'm not a resident of Salem, Massachusetts in 1692 where my neighbors would be whispering among themselves about spectral evidence as they hunt for a suitable stake.

Ethel Esther Etta Karelitz Spector

Of All Sad Words...

At her age excitement is a risky business and so she takes in the deepest breath possible and lets it out slowly in an attempt to quiet her pounding heart. Ethel by age 92 has become a pragmatist and knows better than to succumb to an inflated expectation of seeing her brother for the first time in 65 years. Still, she cannot set aside the possibility. Their twice-yearly phone conversations are always initiated by her but, of course, they would be. She's the big sister and probably the only person in the world who knows his birthday or cares enough to wish him a happy birthday or a healthy new year.

The polite voice of her brother at the other end of the phone line is that of a circuit court judge meticulously describing cases, precedents, rulings, juries, and political infighting. He reviews the convoluted details of the biggest oil and gas case in his state's history. After several other judges have been dismissed, he's tasked with adjudicating this difficult case. He's proud and Ethel is as well. She listens patiently and appreciates the information since she herself was admitted to the Massachusetts State Bar in 1937.

Conversation, however, never turns to personal or family matters. The brother even calls his sister "Ma'am," but having lived out West for all these years, it makes perfect sense to Ethel. He's become a formal and polite man, though he was a devil as a kid when he hid on the roof of his house to throw stones at passers by and willfully pock up the doctor's son with birdshot from his shotgun. He's the kid who says black if his father says white and who charms his mother into hawking her engagement ring to keep him funded at Georgetown's School of Foreign Service in Washington, DC. He's stubborn now and was no different at 20.

Ethel recalls his disappointment then from a letter he wrote to his mother, Molly. Senator Lodge had rested his hand on the young man's shoulder and spoken to him about the impossible path he'd chosen. Unless he was a Cunard family member, the kindly Senator had warned him, he was unlikely to make it in the Foreign Service. A Jew in the Foreign Service? Do yourself a favor, he said, and go on home. Become an honest and honorable lawyer or make a decent living as a schoolteacher.

Ethel understands that it's hard to give up a dream. She wept when she had to close up her office on State Street in 1939 so soon after she'd rented it to assume her housewifely duties. Today, she's just pleased that her brother speaks to her even if it's always on his terms. She remains hopeful because that is her style, and she patiently waits for the day he mentions their brilliant and wise mother so together they can resurrect her with glorious memories. Molly was forever elegant, even as she lay dying. "My jewels," she rasped through labored breaths. "Do not grieve for me but think kindly instead."

Ethel wants to ask her brother if he remembers how Molly read them her favorite story about Cornelia's jewels, her children. She wonders if he agrees that their mother knew she was heading toward the gateway to the end during those five years in the tuberculosis sanatorium. Why else would she have written the script, accepted for a radio show called <u>Heaven – A Dream</u>? Were her smiles complete artifice, an easy cover-up, as she attempted to keep the family from descending into a hellhole of emptiness and fear? Did she bury her head in her pillow and scream in despair the second they left her sickroom? The family was already fragile as she attempted to mediate between her husband and son from her sickbed. It was no secret that she was the glue for the family.

Ethel herself believes their mother would never have wanted them to think anything other than that she intended to get well. Loud and clear, then softer and softer, Molly insisted that with enough rest she would stop coughing. And she grumbled about being stuck in a bed and unable to get permission to walk to the basin to wash her hair. She might then say, "All's well that ends well."

And what did that mean, Ethel wonders, as she's never been able to interpret these quotes to fit into the context of the moment. She craves her brother's answers and opinions, those of a judge after all, because he's accustomed to thinking clearly about difficult matters. Her own decisions were dependent mostly on what cash was available in the family coffers. Living on a tight income with four children and little excess time was complicated. Whether and when to refinish the floors, to buy a newfangled dishwasher or a larger Fridgedaire, to buy or build a ping pong table, all were tricky but hardly cosmic decisions.

Ethel's brother is now the only other person alive who knew and adored their mother. But, while a lot of words bubble over with professional excitement surrounding legal issues of sentencing or jury selection, he never mentions their past. Nor does he ever inquire after her health or that of her family that includes four grown children, nine grandchildren, and six great grandchildren. It remains an unspoken codicil to his contract of silence that she will never mention anyone from the past. Not mother, nor father, aunties, uncles or cousins, and definitely not their Lithuanian family who was murdered in the Holocaust. And never, but never mention his late wife who happened to have the same first name as he and just by coincidence, in a splash of wicked irony, was devoted to her Christian Bible.

In the early 1940s when he brushed away all remnants of his past and his personal history of 17 generations of rabbis to move out West and then marry his strong and beautiful shiksa, it was not acceptable in any circles, except possibly Hollywood, to thumb one's nose at tradition. But he was such a bad boy and determined to have his way, just like the king of England who fell in love with Wallis Simpson, definitely not a beauty but offering the opportunity for Edward to walk away from a stultifying life. Had Ethel's brother been a rabbi, like his grandfathers before him, he would have already known the location of his eternal resting place…in Tel Aviv's Trumpeldor, likely squeezed in between the poet, Bialik, and his grandfather, Baruch Cohen.

Is this brilliant brother stubborn or dedicated, mean-spirited or determined, selfish or principled, narcissistic or simply focused on the road ahead? Like most men, he's a mixture of the devil and an angel, but Ethel forgives him the devil piece, considering him devilish with its much softer implication. She forgives him everything in loving rationalizations, for his was a tough life of poverty, compounded by the incomparable loss of a mother who left home for the hospital one day when he was 15 and never returned.

Ethel looks out her window high above the George Washington Bridge traffic and allows herself the guilty pleasure of thinking back 75 years. The sounds she hears are not honking horns or the screech of brakes but the old mahogany wind up Victrola of those happy days of her teens. The nasal music of Nola scratches out its lively tune through the flared cornucopia horn as her rowdy girlfriends trot at a near gallop around the living room.

Ethel watches video interview of her brother

They're enamored of her tall younger brother and take turns partnering with him to practice their moves.

A barge is being pushed under the bridge toward New York City in water as black as Crystal Lake where her family rented a cabin every summer. Without her hearing aids Ethel wonders how she's hearing the slap of oars as she rows the boat for her brother to go fishing. But this particular early morning, she's complicit as she rows into the middle of the lake not for her brother to cast his reel but to dump evidence. He'd burned the bottom of their mother's favorite pot while making taffy, so he orders Ethel to row straight ahead as he slides the gooey pot overboard like a dead body. She turns toward shore to see if anyone is watching and sees their cottage on the shore with the outhouse high on the hill behind it. As the sun sets behind the river, Ethel remembers, as if it were yesterday, her embarrassment when someone noticed her carrying a roll of toilet paper toward the rickety shack.

The telephone rings to jolt her out of her reverie with its good news. The management at her assisted living residence has reserved its guest room for her brother.

Ethel worries she will swoon when she sees him as an old man. He was such a handsome kid, but won't it be a shock for him to face her as well? Tiny fractures in her tortured back, many of which have healed, pull her face parallel to the floor. What will he think of her at 92 years old, nearly deaf and practically blind? She decides she will sit down to greet him because she's so bent over. Perhaps he won't notice for a while. She won't mention that her pain is nearly intolerable or that her knees have little cartilage. After all the years of walking up and down the hills to the trolley stops or jumping rope with her daughter and her friends, the strong bones of her knees are ground into a bunch of gritty particles.

As her doorbell rings, she's confused for the moment. Maybe her brother has arrived. But as she pushes her walker toward the door at her version of a run, she struggles back into the present. Fortunately it's impossible for her to look up to see the DNR sign taped to the back of her door; and while the note seems cruel for its reminder, it's a kindness. Should any do-gooder paramedics, possibly burdened with youth, attempt to haul her off and hook her up to machines when the endgame is obvious, they'd be disregarding her instructions.

Standing in front of her door and in the hall with a large brownbag of groceries including her salt free bread is her beloved fourth child, a son whom she almost lost in a misaligned pregnancy. He's as good as a daughter and she knows she's blessed. This is the kind of child she can call upon to lift her off the floor where she spent the night waiting until morning so as not to disturb him. This is whom she trusts to help her with the do-not-resuscitate decision.

She sits face to face with him now so she can read his lips while he addresses the business at hand. He asks her renewed blessing before he continues his final, full court press effort to bring her brother to the East Coast to see her. Her son is generous and prepared to offer private jets and cars to make the 89-year-old brother comfortable in his travels. He will offer to collect and escort him all the way.

Ethel responds with, "I see the handwriting on the wall. It is time."

These words document her understanding of reality. Although she doesn't know the name for what's happening to her, she frequently gasps for air, taking in an automatic, life-preserving Cheyne-Stokes breath, and she's completely aware that time is of the essence. Her heart failure doesn't allow her any sodium and drags her into a nearly chronic doze. She certainly cannot travel, so the only question remaining is when and if her brother will arrive for their visit.

Ethel's mind wanders these days more often than she cares to admit. Recently it replayed a screaming scene on the night she came home from the hospital with her firstborn. It was the beginning of the end of her relationship with her brother. She'd been discharged after two weeks and a near death experience after delivering her breech baby amidst great pain and a sea of blood. The doctor was Catholic and had never articulated his personal position in favor of saving the baby's life and letting the chips fall where they may for Ethel.

"And where have you been, you selfish bastard," cried Ethel's husband when her brother finally showed up for the new baby's bris. "Your sister nearly died." That was no exaggeration. And the husband grabbed him by the coat and shoved him out the front door, both of them stumbling to regain balance. "Go to hell!" yelled one of them. And those were the last words spoken between the two men.

Ethel tries to hear her son's words as he shares his specific plans to bring her brother out from his small and dusty corner house in New Mexico. She doesn't know that his favorite sweater is completely peppered with fuzzballs and his flat-soled sneakers are at least a decade old. The blood red of a vicious argument has faded to white. Ethel sees a blinding flash of lightning and smells a distinctive smell of ozone on the night their mother stands on the porch of their three-family house on Clark Street in Malden, Massachusetts. The lightning flies by her to vaporize the family's new crystal radio. Their mother is spared for a few more years before she begins to cough. Does her brother remember that particular terror more than 80 years ago after which their mother gathered them close in a gratitude hug?

"My floater's are giving me the jitters," she tells her son as she recalls seeing the immediate look of horror on her mother's face when the crackling lightning shattered the wondrous little talking machine in the living room.

"Mother! Are you hearing me?" her son asks. The question helps reorient her for the moment.

"Speak up. Please." The batteries in her hearing aids are screaming in torment.

"I'm in another century. I'm not quite together. I'm dilapidated." Her voice is young and rings clear.

"Dilapidated?" her son repeats loud enough for Ethel to hear.

"That's not what I'm trying to say." An empty look clouds her deep set and narrowed eyes as she struggles to find the right word for her near dream state.

Judging from the minutiae of her brother's pontifications, it seems to Ethel that his memory remains first rate while she is losing her vocabulary. Both of them had photographic memories and could recite pages from Ovid or Milton or could recall exactly where on the page the words were written telling of Thetis dipping the infant Achilles into the River Styx. Everyone has a vulnerable spot. Hers is that empty hole when she could no longer visit her mother at the hospital once a week. Her brother has refused to admit to his vulnerable spot, unable or unwilling to revisit the past.

Ethel cannot help herself. The present now is too real. Dementias, Alzheimer's, tiny strokes. The post-herpetic neuralgia on her face from an old case of shingles. But for her the worst is that her junk mail is piling up because she can't figure out exactly what it is, what it says or what it means.

She knows that all control over her formerly orderly and predictable life has vanished and she's now dependent on others for everything. And now she waits for her son to bring her brother to her as if she's the queen requesting his royal presence.

What will her brother think of her, so old and frail, bent and deaf, blind from cataracts and dependent on her walker? They will eat downstairs in the resident dining room at a private table. Perhaps her friends will think she has a boyfriend. Or will it be obvious they are related? Do they still look alike in spite of his bright blue eyes and her dark gypsy eyes? He was the fair child and she was called "black sheep," much to her considerable shame. There was such shame back then, enough to last a lifetime. No wonder her brother refuses to look back.

They have much to talk about and much to decipher, decode, and admit. Will he forgive and forget?

Ethel's mind is unable to stay in the moment and drifts to her two childhood dolls. She reaches automatically for the stuffed doll that was a gift for her 80th birthday. As she winds it up, it begins to belt out its recorded song and move its head and mouth. "Send me a postcard, indicate precisely what you mean to say, yours sincerely, wasting away…will you still need me, will you still feed me, when I'm sixty-four."

Ethel remembers with pride how she takes care of her dolls.

She dresses, feeds, and rocks them in preparation for having her very own babies. She wipes their faces and takes them to the toilet. She tells them to say please and thank you and teaches them how to use a napkin and a pusher for peas. Her favorite babydoll has a soft leather body and blue glass eyes.

One awful morning an acquaintance of her mother's comes to visit them on Clark Street. She has her young daughter with her. This is the only time her darling mother double-crosses her with any demand, especially a cruel one. "You must offer one of your dolls to the little girl who has no doll of her own." When the compliant child, Ethel, asks which one, her mother tells her to let the little girl choose.

⟪⟨

As it turned out:

Ethel could not help but grieve for the rest of her life over the loss of her leather baby doll. But she forgave her mother long ago since that was her style.

Her beloved younger brother refused to make the trip East in spite of the willingness of her son to accompany him and make him as comfortable as possible. He died at age 89 in 2008 and Ethel moved on at age ninety three in 2009. Honoring his brilliance, Colfax County in New Mexico named the new Justice Center after him and his name is carved large in the front of the building. In a generous bequest he left all of his money, $4,000,000, to endow a chair in Evidence at a university law school. While appearing nearly destitute to his neighbors, who rarely caught a glimpse of him or his ancient Bronco, he was unable, or found it unnecessary, to spend money on himself. And he never had the inclination or courage to do his own remembering and recalibrating. Ethel forgave him for he'd suffered, too, and no one except for her knew how terribly. No one attended his burial and only his attorney who happened to hear Ethel's message on his answering machine ever guessed that he had a loving older sister.

Ethel's name is carved in one place only, the granite headstone that marks her grave. Nieces, nephews, caregivers, friends, cousins, and neighbors arrived in Malden, Massachusetts from far and near on a strangely warm and wildly windy day in December of 2009. They eulogized Ethel and followed her body to the cemetery where each of them threw a clod of dirt onto her casket in a last goodbye. Her family tries not to grieve for her but remembers her kindly instead. They work at believing that "all's well that ends well."

The Winter of the Scarf

My stellar intentions and lofty goals often wither when inspected in the sunlight. And my old rationalization that my goals are too sweeping no longer works especially when it comes to wearing my Hermes scarf.

For the briefest moment I blame my late father for burdening me with an inherited perfectionism that stops me dead in my tracks before I can allow a result that's anything less then excellent. For instance, my dad was blessed with the curse of perfect pitch and was stuck listening to the teenage me massacre many classical piano gems. "Play it again!" was his mantra, shouted down the stairs during my practices. That was painful for both of us.

Perhaps it's a leap to suggest that it's my father's fault that not once in 15 years have I worn my glorious scarf. Not once have I knotted it around my neck and stepped outside the safety zone of my house even though I admire it, try it on, pack it for trips and always give it respectful consideration.

I don't need a psychoanalyst to help me deconstruct my

haunting tendencies toward a perfectionist spirit or to shred the self-doubt that keeps me indecisive. Or, maybe I do require long-term effort on a therapy couch? Alone and by myself, am I able to clean out my closet perfectionism and silence my father's shouts, now whispers, to play it again?

⟪ℚ

Fifteen years ago and before I could even pronounce Hermes (Er-Mez'), my brother, in a fit of generosity, selected a gift scarf for me. I recognized its beauty from the start, although in those days I had no knowledge that the uber-silkworms laboring to produce such a weighty silk lived on a farm that Hermes owned in the mountains of Brazil. Neither did I know the year was 1937 when the silk for the first 90-by-90 centimeter Hermes scarves was woven in the company factory in Lyon just before the Nazis overran France. Those colorful scarves fluttered about in stark contrast to soot and explosions amid their owners' fears and ever-present uncertainties around which way the winds of war would blow. Scarf owners carried them along underground as they complied with the warning screams of the air raid sirens. We'll never know how much comfort those original, silky squares provided amidst the jagged landscape of war. In my imagination, utilitarian images of those early scarves knotted tightly around a bloody shrapnel wound or a cache of coveted potatoes overtake the esthetic and limiting notion of the Hermes square as an objet d'art.

I admire my own scarf and recall opening the gift package so long ago. I couldn't have known then that the contents of the flat orange box with its brown grosgrain ribbon would become a thorn in my side rather than a feather in my cap. The packaging was over the top in understated elegance. Inside, the silk square's hand-rolled and hand-stitched edges were as nearly perfect as if finished by machine. Upon quick inspection it was exciting to see dozens of options for aligning the accessory with many clothes in my closet. As I smoothed it into a triangle, my fingers were rough enough to snag the silk, so I used my gardener's lanolin, wiped them clean on a towel, and finished examining the edges.

✺

The Hermes illustrator of my particular scarf had painted rhombus geometrics for the finished print with more than 20 brilliant colors from purply pink to mustard, marine blue, aqua, shades of avocado and Kelly green, all of which created a luscious visual potpourri. Its border of canceled stamps honor technological advancements that include an Hermes Birkin along with at least 25 animals, 15 modes of transportation, and more than 20 olympic sports. The designer selected a blue outer border of nearly three inches to dominate all other colors. However, every color required its own important pass of machinery to print each of the 20 colors and not until 15 hours had elapsed was the printing process completed and the scarf allowed to rest and dry.

My scarf next went into a steam bath to fix the colors and then was washed several times until the silk became soft. A final miracle coat was applied for shine and protection. The completed scarf was delivered to the Paris Hermes boutique on Rue du Faubourg Saint-Honore where my brother happened into the shop after a nice walk from the Eiffel Tower and across the Seine. An efficient and notoriously skilled decision maker, he selected my scarf on a gut feeling, believing it was the most interesting of the offerings in the case after the saleslady shook out several of the twill de soie pieces. Each, of course, had singular merit and as our mother would say indecisively, "Each scarf is as broad as it's long."

Had my brother noticed the fragrances when he entered the shop, he might have brought me Caléche instead of a scarf and my complex challenge would never have reared its head. Instead, for years I've tormented myself with the question of what kind of women have the hubris, daring, and confidence to wear such an intricate piece of art. Surely not the likes of me, the granddaughter of a Russian peasant from Ukraine who owned a single gray woolen babushka to keep her warm and to cover her fair hair of which she was too proud. And then I question why I believe I don't deserve to own the silk square let alone wear it, followed by self-talk, "Where is your self-esteem, Girl"?

Over the years the scarf has gained a stature of mythical proportion as I attempt but fail to coordinate it with something deserving in my wardrobe. Now and then, I hold it against a navy blue or black jacket or a simple dress that "works" though it doesn't exactly do the scarf justice. But then, at the precise moment I settle on a coordinated item of clothing, certain the two will get along well, I shudder at the risk of its loss at this concert, that restaurant, or someone's private party.

It's obvious that the scarf would be diminished in its juxtaposition with any item of clothing I own or any venue other than, perhaps, La Scala. I agree with myself that it's not worth my anxiety. But I know what's really going on and I curse my father's perfectionism.

Further excuses add layer after layer to rationalizations that individually would make sense but en masse are pathological: the weather is too humid to lay heavy silk against my neck; I'm having hot flushes; my neck looks particularly short; I can't locate the little orange book of knots.

Finally, even I am sick of my incessant excuses and have promised myself that this is the winter I'll wear my Hermes scarf. I launch further self-talk. "I'm good enough. I deserve to wear it. My father would love to see the silk against my fair skin." I consider a round of whistling to improve my confidence.

I'm on a forward march and browse women's clothing stores for a blue shell until I discover a sleeveless sweater that seems to be the right shade of blue...until I unwrap it at home. The blues scream foul and I return the sweater for a refund. I baggie a matching marker from my grandchildren's art supplies to carry with me instead of the scarf itself and stuff it ignominiously into the black hole of my purse.

Months pass as I attempt to complete my mission and when I've nearly surrendered to despair, the elusive shade of blue with a tendency toward purple turns up in the form of a cardigan sweater.

I'm feeling confident, but outdoor temperatures have climbed to the mid 80s except at night when I cannot justify wearing my scarf inside a cool movie theater where it might brush up against common seats or the greasy, pop-corned floors of the masses;

neither can I wear it near or with babies or close to the beach where the wind might sweep it into the surf. Nor can I wear it to dinner where salad dressing spatter or worse could stain it for eternity.

The possibility that I have a psychiatric diagnosis such as a phobic personality disorder teases me. God forbid. I steel myself and, though anxious, I prepare to meet the challenge of "the donning of the scarf." I'm truly and unequivocally committed. All I have to do is decide which knot to use and whether to put it around my neck, my head or my waist since I'd never risk dangling it off my purse. I enter the Hermes website for information on tying the scarf and my heart sinks when I discover the recommendation that the scarf be worn with the Hermes scarf ring for "best results."

The price tag on both models of scarf ring slows me down, but I'm now convinced that the scarf is nothing without the shiny ring with its Hermes lettering. I must own the correct ring designed especially for the scarf. But now the problem is not just how to explain this reckless need to my brother, the gifter, an out-of-the-box thinker who considerately suggested I use my napkin ring in place of the Hermes scarf ring. Out of respect, I try on that walnut napkin ring but it trivializes my gorgeous scarf and makes me feel as though I'm wearing my dinner napkin on top of my sweater tablecloth.

So I'm back to square one and ponder which scarf ring to order, the shiny titanium that would go well with my white gold jewelry or the yellow gold that goes with my yellow gold jewelry?

I've exhausted myself with waffling and refuse to allow this alarming, uncharming charade to continue for another 15 years. So I have several choices. I can remove the scarf from my view by destroying it or I can re-gift it to a stylish young woman with a long neck. Since neither of those choices makes me happy, I've settled on the only decision possible given the circumstances.

My silk square is at the frame shop with specific handling instructions. I am relieved to have trapped this needling symbol of my perfectionism and existential threat to my serenity. No longer a torment and something that I "should" be wearing, my Hermes scarf will hang securely on the wall where I will view it as I would a spectacular painting. I've accepted the reality that a scarf of this caliber isn't destined to be worn by me because I don't have what it takes in terms of wardrobe, neck length, body temperature, social life or personal style. It would take more years than I have left on earth to convince myself that I deserve to drape this twill de soie on my body, with or without the anneaux de carres.

I promise I'll be content, as its proud owner, to see the splashes of color on my wall where it's protected from contamination, spills, splatters, loss, or theft.

Finally, I'm at peace in the knowledge that I'm cut from the same piece of cloth as my father.

One Door Closes

T he January sunset promised to be spectacular because mackerel clouds had floated toward the West Coast on a wind from a distant storm. I was forever hopeful that today would be the day I'd finally witness the Green Flash. I'd been waiting and watching the sky above the outline of Catalina Island for years hoping for a quick glimpse of the elusive phenomenon. I didn't understand anything about optics, prisms or refractions, but I didn't want to leave this world without having seen the Green Flash. I rushed out the door and down Heliotrope toward Lookout Point in Corona del Mar. With five minutes to spare before the spiritual experience of the sunset, I was moving quickly.

The bluff was 80 yards away and six houses down the slight hill and across the street. Houses were built on skinny lots in Corona del Mar each with 30- or 40-foot frontage so it was but a hop, skip and a jump to my favorite bench. From that bench cut into the hillside about 10 steps below street level, I'd observed many group baptisms where life would begin anew for everyone dipped backwards, nosed pinched, soaked and saved. I remembered the most romantic beach scene from my childhood filmed right there on the beach below.[1] Deborah Kerr in her one piece bathing suit entwined with Burt Lancaster on the sand while the imagined cameraman tiptoed about as unobtrusively as possible. I would carefully wait for the exact moment the sun dropped behind Catalina Island. Then, without a discernable flash, I'd say, "Well, maybe tomorrow," although I couldn't wait for eternity.

Two houses from mine a stranger was coming through the Campbell's[2] old gate, and the expression on her face told me that all was not well in the world. She was too reserved, too hesitant, too regal for the beach as she opened that gate that had seen a lot of activity since the 1940s when the cottage was built. Only three houses existed in the neighborhood then as Mrs. Campbell realized she could no longer tolerate the intense worry about her teenage son sleeping on the beach when he came from Pasadena on weekends to surf "the wedge." The waves themselves could be frightening coming in as they did at an odd angle to the beach, so why double-tempt the fates, Mrs. Campbell thought. Unsavory characters had been known to harass young people. So, that was why the Campbells built

---

[1] From Here to Eternity

[2] Mrs. Campbell, until well into her 90s, continued to drive the distance from Pasadena over the heavily traveled expressways of Southern California to Corona del Mar, where she hiked down the hill to China Cove. She pulled on her bathing cap and swam in the cove, calling the water "brisk," and then hiked her way back up the 100 plus steps to the top of the bluffs and on to her cottage. I wonder if Mrs. Campbell's tradition of the swim in the numbing cold water helped her survive the loss of her daughter, Pixie.

the cottage on their skinny rectangle of paradise and it was as good a reason as any other I'd heard.

I nodded and said hello to the stranger just out of the gate, and since she was obviously heading to the bluffs, we walked the rest of the way together. "My" bench overlooking Pirate's Cove was empty so we sat together and struck up the most superficial of conversations. "Oh you're a friend of Mrs. Campbell's. Nice to meet you, Shirley." Then, "How nice you're enjoying her cottage by the sea." "Oh, you're from Breckenridge. Colorado? And you were best friends with Pixie, Mrs. Campbell's daughter?"

Then Shirley's eyes welled up with tears as she told me she'd attended Pixie's funeral just that day and it was a rotten day for her. I reached for her hand as I thought about what it would feel like to lose my best friend. Who would echo my joys and fears and who would talk me down when I was about to go over the edge? I need my girlfriends.

Pixie was a scientist, Shirley told me, studying ovarian cancer and in a cruel irony she herself had succumbed to it. I could muster only the most trivial words of condolence. But sitting there together on that bench watching and hoping for that elusive Green Flash provided comfort to Shirley and to me, the intruder.

Soon after our first meeting, I showed Shirley a place on a deserted bluff further south that I'd recently discovered. We brought a picnic to the wild site that overlooked the Pacific Ocean, a place more beautiful when shared. No one was around and the cliff was straight down. I set up my collapsible little table on the precipice and set a vase with a flower on top. I hoped that

Shirley would begin to feel a little more secure about being left in the world without her dearest friend.

Shirley insisted that when one door closed, another opened. This door just happened to be a squeaky gate.

Freda Warrington and Freda Warrington

Doppleganger

One definition of doppelganger: A literary technique by which a character is duplicated (usually in the form of an alter ego, though sometimes as a ghostly counterpart) or divided into two distinct, usually opposite personalities.

This Freda Warrington was cynical at times and suspicious at other times but masqueraded as the quintessential Jewish mother. The other Freda Warrington was as sweet and naïve as tupelo honey but wore Dracula capes and purple streaked hair. We found each other in a Berlin bookstore and became the most natural of doppelgangers.

The other Freda and I, while an oddly opposite couple, were unlike Felix and Oscar who nearly pecked each other to death. We were instead like a pair of cheerleaders without the squeals and excessive hugging. The novelty of having found each other and then discovering we were each writing novels was spooky. In fact, her novels were spooky because her genres were Vampire and Fantasy. Her language ebbed and flowed with ethereal and gorgeous descriptions while my language reflected the real world with its share of brutalities, abuse, and loss. Sometimes, too, our worlds overlapped, with her created aetherials being the counterpoint to the magical moments in my life.

While the Other Freda strolled Bradgate Park or Robin Hood's woods, breathing in the blooming surprises in every cranny or the rotting possibilities under every root, I sat in my private therapy office with its well-worn sofa. That's where I met with the sick and wounded, the place where I sifted and reframed rantings, tears and obsessions as best I could. This was the place to leave secrets that were too dangerous for the group therapy room.

❦

The other Freda arrived from England for our first meeting in the United States just in time for a surprise Ben and Jerry's birthday party for my husband who was fanatical about his ice cream. As a matter of fact, Ben and Jerry had been invited but were allegedly in South America. They sent along good wishes, a personally autographed Ben and Jerry T-shirt, and 20 coupons for pints of free ice cream.

The other Freda Warrington and her boyfriend were happy to be among us and we all judged the party an auspicious beginning to our friendship. Guests to whom I introduced her ranged from mildly amused to incredulous since we were not exactly a pair of Jane Smiths. We were distinguished from each other not only by our accents, mine being Bostonian and hers being British, but also by our facial features. She had the thin look of an Irish lass and I the round appearance of a Russian peasant. We were both petite with huge smiles that night as we enjoyed the attention.

My reciprocal visit to England the following autumn was

a let down only because I'd ratcheted up my expectations. The other Freda's stationery depicted a graphic of a blackbird and the header was "Blackbird Cottage." The lettering was perfect for the writer of vampire and fantasy novels as was the rest of the romantic address. However, when we arrived in Castle Gresley, in Derbyshire, England and finally located the other Freda's cottage, I was gravely disappointed. She lived in a simple two-story row house without a thatched roof. What was I expecting? A raven at her front door perched on a stile shrieking "Nevermore?" I admit to being the Freda who's always looking for magic and then gets suspicious if she finds it.

The Freda of Blackbird Cottage is a gentle soul who loves frogs and stuffed animals and sleeps in a bed the size of Sleeping Beauty's. Her mind flits, dodges and weaves as she creates her novels in other lands, sometimes half in and half out of this world. People are not always entirely human but manage to have compelling traits and defects of character just as if they inhabited the real world of London economics or Wall Street. But they often live elsewhere in the other Freda's novels.

"So, who is the beauty and who is the beast in this twosome?" I wondered for a long time. Is one of us the Superego and one, the Id? Which is the ghostly counterpart to the other? Can we mix things up and reverse roles as good cop doppelganger and bad cop doppelganger in the therapy room? Do we belong in the other Freda's supernatural novels? Or should we settle into the therapy room...as patients?

The truth may reside in the simple concept of probability and the fact that there are likely some other Freda Warringtons in the world, Fredas who write and Fredas who travel. Whether or not there's any universal message to be found in our intersection at the towering display of <u>A Taste of Bloodwine</u> in that Berlin bookstore is no longer important. And whether or not our meeting was Someone's Grand Plan with the American Freda seeing math and the British Freda seeing magic or vice versa, it makes no difference. We're not literary creations but two women with two distinct and opposite personalities. And we certainly qualify as doppelgangers, familiar ones at that, since our relationship has endured now for 25 years.

It's safe to say that we both are comforted to have learned from the wisdom of Buckaroo Banzai. No matter where you go, there you are. Tacking on our personal tidbits of wisdom, we add that it's helpful if you like yourself and lagniappe if you like each other.

Inevitable?

My husband called home from a business trip in the Far East before he left for his favorite sukiyaki lunch. I was tired from Blue Birds, T-Ball, cupcake baking, and the nuisance of locating a male in the community who knew how to light the furnace in our attic. I was resentful as I held down the fort so he could traipse halfway around the world to be entertained by geishas and ferried around in limousines. Our children were tucked into bed and everyone in my world, I believed, was safe. I ignored the clicks from the new feature of call waiting not just once, but twice.

My friend Theresa had been calling me for help but it wasn't until the next morning that I knew why. Her husband, Stan, was dead and she needed me to deliver his best suit to the funeral home on Route 59, north of Houston. Although he'd been hospitalized in a psychiatric hospital for depression, Stan appeared to be improving after electroshock therapy treatment. So I was stunned to hear that he'd been taken from the psychiatric ward on a pass and allowed to roam alone in a big store. It was in that impersonal cold space that he gently asked the salesman to look at a gun on the wall behind the counter. And then he asked again, very quietly, for that was his way, to see a box of bullets. Stan loaded quickly, opened his mouth and pulled the trigger. He had plans but hadn't mentioned them to a soul, except maybe his God.

My belief that I was a grownup was challenged again as I tried to bear up long enough to do the simple, though macabre, errand asked of me. I drove to the funeral home on autopilot while my thoughts raced. The air in the car seemed too damp and heavy to inhale. What should I have done to help? Shame on me, his good friend. We'd only had a few visits recently and I wonder if he felt like an outcast among us especially since he'd lost much of his memory due to the induced seizures of electoconvulsive therapy (ECT).

On that drive to deliver Stan's best suit for his burial and to bring home his personal effects, I was filled with overwhelming feelings of guilt. In those days I was young enough to be unaware that when someone decides to kill himself, it's often a mindset no one can interrupt.

At the funeral home, I traded Stan's best suit for a clean manila envelope. It was only instinct that made me bring it to my house instead of straight to his wife, Theresa. I took a deep breath before I pulled up the metal tabs on the envelope and dumped the contents onto my kitchen table. For once I'd made a good call.

Pocket change, a money clip, a comb, a thin wallet, and shattered eyeglasses. No clues or notes existed and nothing significant to tell the story of Stan, lovely refined Stan, the kind of man who looks directly at you and listens when you speak. He was the kind of man who might ask a follow-up question so you knew for certain he'd heard you. And now before me on the table his ugly suicide was evident as dried blood contaminated each and every small relic, from his comb to his wedding band to the ruins of his eyeglasses. I used paper towels and cotton to clean up one piece after another before returning each item to the envelope. It became my secret and final gift to Stan, my mitzvah to him, that I sanitized the contents of that envelope. For how could the people who loved Stan the most bear to see his life's blood splattered on everything? Stan after all was a son, a father, a lover and a husband.

I can see myself, all those years ago, weeping at my kitchen table as I wiped down the remains of his young life. Weeping, wiping and talking. Self-talk is something I do and this time it was out loud. "Stan, why did you leave Theresa such a legacy? And your children? And your mother and father? Couldn't you have spared all of us this pain? Did you really need to exit this world now? And with a gun in your mouth?" And then with my selfishness, hurt, and fear diminishing with everything back in the envelope, "You must have been in such pain, feeling so hopeless, so completely overwhelmed, so miserable." And finally to myself, "Where the hell were you, Miss Smarty? Making cookies for Bluebirds? You couldn't make time for a visit? You didn't look up to notice your friend's excruciating pain while you were creaming the butter and sugar?" And my weeping turned to crying. "Surely, you could have baked him your yogurt cake. You know, the one he loved with the pineapple? Maybe your Passover sponge cake with all the eggs? You could have talked to him about the priesthood, validated his dreams to enter the seminary. You might have tried to suggest a way forward out of the conflict of his marriage and into the comforting world of the spirit." I can be tough on myself for the mitzvah, such as it was, had accomplished little, and in those days I had this grandiose notion that there was a fix for everything.

I couldn't stand myself as I comforted with one hand and then backhanded with the other. "Stan, you were a man of God... though God would not be pleased after this selfish little stunt. Here's Theresa taking in boat people from Vietnam, and now you've really put that operation into limbo. Was that your plan?"

No one will ever know what was in Stan's mind or the enormity of his pain although at that age, in my 30s, I had the audacity to believe I was both sensitive and educated. The gentle Stan chose death over life.

I still can't help wondering if it was inevitable.

Thank You, Warden

Joanie and I needed special dispensation from our warden to room together my sophomore year and her junior year. We weren't in a prison but resided in an ivory-towered college for a four-year respite from the outside world, a time when daisy-chained nymphets and everyone else who had the courage to matriculate were free to mine the depths of Knowledge.

I can only guess that Warden Miss Drouillet had her own reasons for keeping the jaded upperclassmen away from us sophomores. Perhaps she feared students like us would become a precedent that interrupted her strategic plan for firmly cemented bonds within each class. I only know for certain that Joanie and I arrived at the appointed time in our best skirts for the dreaded meeting with the Warden. We were immediately ushered into her large office. Joanie was demur as she crossed her gorgeous legs, lowered her curly auburn head of hair and fixed her doe eyes on the warden. I was shaken by the gravity of the event as well as by Miss Drouillet herself whose skin matched her tweedy gray and brown clothes. She was a Pre-Raphaelite vision (Art 101) in austerity with an

Freda and Joanie in Rome, Italy and in Tossa del Mar, Spain

ecru blouse opened at the throat. Her spectral presence alone should have made us withdraw our request and bolt, but Joanie and I had become very fond of each other. We desperately wanted to room together and continue our close relationship.

I recall the substance of the meeting only as a warning about academic standing and since mine was poor, I was forewarned to be wary. I turned red in the steam-heated room and lied as I promised I would swear off having too much fun.

In hindsight, I wonder if our application was approved because of Joanie's tic. I'd stopped noticing it, but I believe Ms. Drouillet refused to be blamed if Joanie's tic became more pronounced because of a rejection. In those days tics were thought to be a result of some deep-seated psychological trauma, a gestalt manifestation of an inner demon, with Joanie's particular issue being the sudden death of her father when she was 12. While Joanie and I never discussed such a calculated theory, I now believe it was a done deal when we walked into the Warden's office. Just the potential threat of triggering an exacerbation of Joanie's tic had made our day.

That tic went like this: Joanie's thin left shoulder would rise up toward her left ear while her redheaded mop tilted charmingly toward that side. The tic was always present although it seemed to slow down while she ate. But, then, everything slowed down while Joanie ate. She chewed and chewed while time stood still and everyone left the dining room. Even the student garbage scrapers standing over the slop hole behind the kitchen counter, pulled off their hairnets and walked out while Joanie continued her thorough mastication. She would not and could not be rushed, and no one ever asked Joanie to speed up her chewing or to swallow faster. We accepted the oddity as integral to Joanie's personality (Psych 101). Lento on the chewing and molto giocoso on the laughter (Music 105).

Joanie and I established a Mutt and Jeff routine, a Laurel and Hardy tit-for-tat, and our friends enjoyed watching our interaction. Had we not liked men so much, we would have made a perfect marriage. Joanie was tall and willowy with shapely calves and beautiful feet. I was short and petite with black hair and green eyes. She was daring and I was not; I had no noticeable family dysfunction except for perfectionism, but she with her blended family had plenty; she loved foreign policy and I thought I loved people. She took a little yellow pill at night to help her mornings ablutions while I carried a brown bottle with a dropper for opium drops to calm my inner somersaults. Her boyfriends were from Yale and mine were from Princeton and Tufts. But, Joanie had a wicked sense of humor and so did I. And that is how we were simpatico. Laughter trumped all in our Swiss cheese relationship.

After Joanie graduated and before I headed into my senior year, I meticulously planned our summer trip using the guidebook, Europe on $5 a Day. I'd made hotel reservations, purchased Eurail student passes and wheels for our luggage, and even bought shoes to match dresses coordinating with the yellow cover I'd made for my travel bible by Frommer. But, few of my carefully conceived plans were not adjusted or ultimately scrapped as we missed trains, remained in places too long or not long enough. We dragged our suitcases from Belgium to Paris and a shopping spree in Galeries Lafayette, on to Nice while picking up dangerous men on the train, then to Barcelona on a crowded train, and to Monaco where we dreamed of meeting shipping magnates or a Grimaldi cousin on the campus of the Rainier Palace, whichever came first. From there we went to Rome where we enjoyed a lovely week wined and dined by Enrico and Federico, another set of pickups; then to Brindisi and then Greece to party at a friend's in Athens before and after picking our way over the steaming hot rubble of the Acropolis. As girls from the Ivory Tower, we were repulsed by the hole in the concrete floor of the misnomered ladies' room at the bus stop en route to Patras. We made it to Florence and on to Lucerne, then Frankfurt and over the rough English Channel where I spent my 21st birthday vomiting in an overnight berth. By then, after the two months of being together 24/7, Joanie and I were getting sick of each other. She had little sympathy for me that night as I played the victim, consigned as I was to a most unpleasant transition to adulthood.

But our relationship rallied in time for pheasant under glass and a bird's nest soup the next night in London. My most salient memory is that of the next morning when a career waitress looked through to the true me, some dumb college kid...in yellow for Gods sake...on holiday between her junior and senior year. That's why ordering kippers for breakfast at the Harwich stop after being quizzed by immigration, was laughable. I was probably still green from the night on the English Channel. "Kippers?" she asked. And then again, "Kippers?" In spite of her Cockney accent, her supercilious tone hammered home the point that she knew that I didn't know what I was doing, never mind how to debone a kipper.

Although we spent a serene week in Bloomsbury in awe of Virginia Woolf and her crowd, we were soon off to Golders Green to meet Joanie's current boyfriend's mother and then to hunker down one cold night in my distant cousin's empty flat where we had no shillings for the heater meter. In truth we didn't learn until later that such a piece of archaic machinery existed in the basement.

Our financial resources were running out despite our austerity budget, but at least we, by now, felt cosmopolitan. We'd learned how to brush off a flasher in the London Tube when he opened his trench coat. We'd returned a small smile to Mona Lisa, explored Montmartre, stepped over Dutch dogs' poo by the Herengracht canal en route to Annelies Marie Frank's hiding place, and experienced the acoustical pleasures of <u>Aida</u> at the Baths of Caracalla. We even fancied ourselves curatorial wonders with a pious outrage at "Night Watch" hanging in its trivialized location at the Rijksmuseum.

By late August of 1964 I left Joanie at Heathrow and flew home for my senior year at college. She headed back to Paris to learn French as an au pair and, as such, was forced to absorb the intricacies of escarole versus arugula versus endive. She fell in love with Nicky, a handsome young desk clerk from South Africa with whom she had a mad love affair that ultimately didn't work out. When she returned at age 29 to a job in Washington, DC, she was sadder and wiser.

◦◦

I was married with one child when a call came from Joyce, my dearest childhood friend. "Freda," was all she needed to say. The tone of her voice told me it was a serious call and not a surprise chat. She'd wanted to warn me before I read the news in the <u>Vassar Quarterly</u>, our alumnae magazine. Joanie was dead from a crash in her Volkswagon as she careened off a street exit in a rainstorm.

When I finally had the courage to try to contact her mother to talk, I couldn't locate her since her last name was different from Joanie's. And 10 years later when I did find her, I asked if she'd like me to send her my pictures of Joanie from our trip. She said no and it was a firm and unequivocal no. It had taken her a long time to get past Joanie's death, she told me, and she didn't want any reminders.

How could she not want to gather to her breast every shred of proof of the existence of her beautiful girl? Did she pack up the details of her daughter's life and dump them all? Wouldn't she like to see how the young men surrounded Joanie on the beach at Tossa del Mar? How they stood on their heads for her? Wouldn't she care to take a peek at how Carlo in Greece responded to Joanie's misty-eyed look when she put in her contact lenses? I asked her mother in my own mind, wasn't it you who rocked her and spooned tapioca into that baby mouth, and wasn't it you who comforted her when her father died from a heart attack?

Her mother sounded angry at me on the phone for barging into her life out of the blue. Or maybe she was furious at Joanie. I didn't understand it then but now that I'm old, I've learned that everyone deals with grief in her own way. Some people talk it to death so as to remember the happy details of the lost life, and others, like Joanie's mom, package it away, wrapping it securely to tuck into a crevice. It's a personal choice about how best to survive the snuffing out of a dear life.

Myself? I choose to remember a smiling, thoughtful, and freckled-faced girl with the grace of a ballerina who loved me, her green-eyed, pink-cheeked roommate. I regret that she didn't know my children or grandchildren, and I'm sad we didn't have a future together, for we'd invested a lot of love and energy into our relationship. Our laughter would likely have continued until our final days. Instead, what remains is a class tree on the Vassar campus growing slowly in Joanie's memory, my fading Kodak photos of our summer, and a pair of gypsy earrings sent to me from Paris and now a prime target for our granddaughters in dressup.

And there's this vignette, too, of my perfect guidebook attempt to construct our moment together in history and how none of it played out as planned.

My father's drugstore scale for weighing cocaine and herbs

Another Man's Treasure

My father said he harbored relics from his old drug store because he never knew when he would need them. But that was only half the story.

His stash included an assortment of large and small glass measures, an eyecup, one oversized, biscuit porcelain mortar and pestle, weights, two scales and one giant tome of 1792 pages, the 21st edition from 1926 of the <u>Dispensatory of the United States of America</u>. Buried within its pages were the compounding secrets for creating suspensions, salves, pills and suppositories.

One of his scales weighed cocaine and powders from herbs, barks, pods, and roots and the other scale was for peppermints, jellybeans, horehound drops, and ribbon candy. This paraphernalia, considered debris by my mother, was the source of constant aggravation for her as it occupied an entire bookcase in the study of my parents' retirement apartment. Space was limited there unlike in their former house on Elmore Street with a basement and a two-room attic for storage. But until I willingly pledged to provide these drugstore artifacts a safe and secure home, my father, Asher, refused to divest himself of them. Now that I'd agreed, Mother was pleased as punch and thanked her lucky stars that I wanted them for my own.

"The inspector from the Massachusetts Department of Weights and Measures showed up on schedule every year to test and calibrate my scales," Dad said, pointing to the glass cover protecting the delicate balances in the wooden box and the green label on the top that read "Do Not Remove."

He reminisced about how he made the yearly inquisitor a cherry coke, no ice, as he sat on the round red stool at the soda fountain. Those general inspections, he said, were necessary to protect the public from an unscrupulous pharmacist and also from formulations that were corrupted and potentially deadly. "The specific properties of such ingredients as cynara artichoke for treatment of rheumatism must be precisely weighed or the medicine could become a part of a larger problem," he explained. And while those days happened a century ago and despite the leech fad and the liberal use of cocaine and laudanum, "safe and effective" were noble aspirations for the practice of medicine. The inspector's job was serious.

My father was among the first of his generation to use his pragmatic good sense to counter the voodoo of those days. He was suspicious of the medical world that sent off tuberculosis patients to the seashore to rest and take in the damp salt air. He'd watched his mother-in-law, my grandmother Molly, deteriorate under those conditions and knew there was much more to this dreaded disease, just as he knew it wasn't sensible to bleed a weak and dying person. While "do no harm" was the good intention of medicine even then, it was a rational man who served that cherry coke to the inspector and who refused to be a partner in anything that made no sense. In fact, he should have been the infection control czar at a large hospital because of his compulsive penchant for hand washing and fingernail scrubbing. Clean hands were as important to him as the otherworldly ultraviolet light hovering over his Coca Cola glasses lined up behind the soda fountain.

While the Pure Food and Drugs Act of 1906 was designed to prohibit adulterated drugs and false branding, there were no committees and no black-boxed pharmaceuticals. And lobbyists or politics surrounding the modern construct of Big Pharma didn't exist. Pharmacists in those days studied their six-inch thick dispensatories, books that held all the magical answers to treating illness and disease. They became expert at rolling pills and making suppositories and could answer general questions for people who sought guidance for dandruff, rash, eczema and birth control.

Among the most improbable of crises was an occurrence that perfectly demonstrated how easy it is to create your own hell. On a beautiful April day, my frantic mother raced the three blocks to the drugstore, me in my baby carriage with my older brother hanging onto its side bar for dear life. Dad was singing an aria in the back room, probably Puccini, while grinding something white into a powder when he heard the commotion up front. I'm told that I screamed hysterically in the carriage as they undid the restraining straps while Mother directed attention to a small stack of cheerios stuffed up my nose. My father, a quick thinker and a wanna-be doctor who was unable to squeeze under the Jewish quota for medical school, gave me a pinch of snuff. I immediately rewarded his ingenuity with a sloppy sneeze that popped out my favorite snack.

That event ended as quickly as it began but not before my father asked my mother in a somewhat accusatory tone, "Where were you, Mother, while she was packing her nose?"

Bristling at the implication that she wasn't minding the children properly, she said, "Asher, while trying to make you a treat with this empty ration book, I was flipping through Women's Day to look for the recipe for refrigerator bread pudding." Mother then brandished in the air and with dramatic flourish the thin little book with few remaining ration stamps. "Then I noticed two articles on the Equal Rights Amendment and both Judge Kenyon and Miss Politzer made some good points."

I was squirming with boredom and wanted to be released from the carriage while Mother described her infatuation with Victory Garden, the rug that took first place in the magazine's hooking competition.

Today, having subjected myself to my own children, I know that no parent should blame another for anything stuffed anywhere. Kids stuff forks into electrical outlets, beans in their ears, and themselves into cabinets and worse. My granddaughter's friend was found to have inhaled "accidentally" a Barbie doll shoe that caused chronic infections until an X-ray uncovered the culprit. An incredulous radiologist was heard to say, "Is that a shoe? I believe that's a shoe. In fact it's a high heel."

In the grand scheme of things the Cheerio debacle was not cosmic.

My father was asking, "What about this? Who would even want it?" He'd pulled open the top dresser drawer to dig out his Rho Pi Phi fraternity pin edged exquisitely with seed pearls. He was very proud of his fraternity that was founded with friendship and service at its heart rather than exclusivity.

With all the misery in the world the week he and Mother were engaged, I can imagine them and his pharmacy school friend, Eddie Duchin, swinging at the Ritz, Dad wearing his tiny two part pin on his jacket lapel and Eddie in his tuxedo. Both busy men were likely oblivious to the bad news of the day. Eddie's band was playing and Mother and Dad were dancing. A million miles away were floods in San Francisco, a prison riot in South Carolina, 600 marooned passengers on board the President Hoover, 11 infant deaths in a Chicago hospital epidemic, and, worst of all, the Japanese sinking of a U. S. gunboat called the Panay. Love trumped all and the young couple was focused only on the future together. The band leader watched them with a sad envy.

Dad couldn't afford an expensive engagement dinner at the Ritz that cold December night in 1938, but he ordered two glasses of pink champagne. Eddie left the band playing his hit tune De-Lovely for a dance with Mother. "Hey Ethel," he whispered. "I need you more than Asher does," and he may have given her a squeeze at her narrow waist. The charming Eddie was really saying, "My baby boy needs a mother." But knowing my mother and how quickly the color arose in her ruddy complexion after a little wine, she turned a bright shade of crimson. And with a heart as big as hers, she must have gotten teary-eyed. Everyone knew how he lost his beautiful young wife five days after she gave birth.

Dad was proud of my pretty Mother and her law degree. He never found out what his buddy had whispered and life went on. And now Eddie had been dead far too long when Dad at 80 years of age was preparing to part with his scales and fraternity pin.

I held up the pin to show Dad how nice the pin would look on the lapel of my jacket.

The tightness in his jaw disappeared as he relaxed in relief knowing that his treasures wouldn't be tossed carelessly into the Goodwill bin along with his old clothes.

꿍

Clarence Marsh, our next-door neighbor who had moved in with Bertha to live in blissful sin, was also anxious about letting go of his valuables. He was born in 1899 and was well into his 80s on the day I was visiting my parents and he'd stopped by for a cup of tea. His partnership with Bertha was a blessing that even my proper mother recognized for the true happiness it created. But Bertha had died and left him. "I miss her terribly. She's left me for good," he said. He spoke with such genuine sorrow, unusual for men of his generation who would rarely be caught wearing their hearts on their sleeves.

Clarence, still a tall man, stumbled to his feet half way through his A&P cup of tea with honey to run next door to grab something he'd just remembered. He returned with six newspapers from the Civil War. They'd belonged to his grandfather and his father had saved them. Clarence had inherited them and squirreled them onto a shelf in the back corner of a closet, valuable as a tangible connection to his grandfather. Now they were a gift for me and he could stop ruminating about losing them in a rushed crisis cleanout. Am I rewriting history when I recall a look of relief on the face of Clarence with me now a willing custodian?

Those old newspapers were expensive. They cost three cents each in 1864 compared to a penny in 1933 for a postcard and two cents for Women's Day in 1943. Still it was a small price to pay to catch up on the progress of the Generals Grant and Sherman whose battle outcomes determined the life or death of the Union. For lagniappe those three cents brought a reader the latest remedies for catarrh and kidney gravel as well as scandalous muckraker reports such as the pollution of the local East Boston neighborhood air from a bone burning operation.

Over that cup of tea, Clarence deadpanned that his personal story of World War I wasn't too exciting because he hadn't been shot. Yet he went on describing his life as a newly enlisted sailor and rolled it out as if it were yesterday instead of 1918 and 1919. He'd been a gunner in the Navy on a supply ship that traveled back and forth to France from America and laughed about how rich he felt on his salary of $55 a month. No expenses except for chewing gum and furlough cash. Compared with the 35 cents an hour for a nine-hour day at the ice warehouse, Clarence felt not only rich, but lucky.

On November 12, 1918 Clarence's and my hometown of Arlington, Massachusetts were on a high. The newspapers screamed "VICTORY! PEACE! Liberty For The World." The

War had ended at 6 a.m. the day before and in grand celebration a parade was to form up at the corner of Park and Mass Avenues, the location 20 years later of my father's drug store. It would march toward Arlington Center and down Broadway to Marathon. The Boy Scouts and Girl Scouts, the Boy's Brigade and Camp Fire Girls, the Red Cross and the rest of the town would be outdoors to celebrate the end of the war with a band concert at Spy Pond Field at 3:30 p.m. and community sing-alongs. And at night in the Town Hall starting at 7:30 patriotic addresses were planned, along with more singing.

No one was happier than Clarence though he wasn't in town to wave to the crowds. He was in France waiting for his ship to be piloted up the Gironde River when the news had arrived the day before: *la guerre est fini*.

When he'd enlisted as a young man of 19, Clarence and the other volunteers received a free lobster lunch at Dini's. That cost the government at least $1.95 and it trumped by a mile scrod or mackerel as a main course. On a full stomach he was in a good mood to be sworn in at the Boston Naval Shipyard after which he was to go home and wait to be called up. That cable arrived on December 7, but Clarence was really miserable and swollen with the mumps. He cabled that he was sick and couldn't come. The return cable read, "Report. Bring mumps." Clarence laughed as he recalled the no-nonsense cable but did as he was told and landed in Hingham at the Navy Yard.

That winter was especially brutal and the water in the bay froze so Clarence and his buddies walked across the ice from Bumpkin Island in Boston Harbor to civilization for Saturday night furloughs. "I wish I'd had my father's bicycle to get around in those days," he said. He looked through the venetian blinds and out the window of our dining room to the street where I learned to ride my big brother's Schwinn with the ominous cross bar.

Clarence said, "My father used to tell me about my grandfather's Speedmaker that needed a set of feet to propel it forward. But Father's bicycle was a newfangled Velocipide, a contraption that could really cover some ground."

He unfolded his crumbling newspapers. "This <u>Boston Daily Evening Traveler</u> was printed the same year my granddad went to New Haven to pick up that crazy Speedmaker and bring it home on trains that connected here and there. Granddad told us he was too old to fight for the Union." Clarence shook his head and finished his thought, "But he was strong enough to slog through

The candy scale

road ruts on two wheels."

On the front page of the Saturday June 4, 1864 edition resting on top of the others the bold letters, F-E-M-A-L-E, caught my eye. "Strengthening Cordial to correct all disorders incidental to the female sex, specifically good for the uterus and a valuable agent for all derangements of the reproductive organs." With my middle-aged jaundiced eye, it seemed sensible to dose those of us deranged in the nether region with a relaxing cordial.

Clarence pulled his glasses off the top of his head to set them down on his nose. He read, "We can see nothing in the accounts we have of General Grant's operations that are not of the most heartening character."

He interrupted himself. "No one I ever knew, on either side, wanted war." While on a reconnaissance mission and looking for German airplanes, he and his commanding officer found a stranded German pilot. He asked him, "Wolfgang, vas ist los?" and the pilot answered, "Nicht mehr benzin." They exchanged names addresses and then filled the German's tank with enough fuel to let him fly back to Belgium thereby creating an oxymoronic civilized bubble in the middle of the brutal war to end all wars.

Clarence must have told his story dozens of times to eager listeners like myself, mostly ignorant of the details of both World Wars. He made me think.

"I didn't exactly see the trenches but heard enough to know it was horrifying in there. The stink of trench foot and icy water up to your knees. Our boys were told to keep their feet clean and dry." He laughed at the impossible nature of the command. "Now how the heck would they manage that?"

Clarence continued, "When we were running supplies back and forth across the ocean, we were dumping bodies overboard. Not from gangrene but from the influenza pandemic. Dozens of bodies from each ship in our convoy were slipped into the black waters of the Atlantic." Clarence eyes misted noticeably at the recollection. "That was enough dying for me."

I suspected that in the old man's mind the horrors of war were conflated with the terror of the pandemic. Those old memories were no-doubt being revisited now that Bertha was gone. Who would be next? And when would it be his turn? Was the churning ocean a good resting place for eternity? Or would a spot beside Bertha be more comfortable?

Clarence poked his glasses up higher onto the bridge of his nose and continued reading the news from 1864. "Anything is possible in war, and it is our duty to have both sides of the picture constantly in our minds. Fortune, that name for the unknown combinations of infinite power, was wanting to Napoleon, and without her aid the designs of man are like bubbles on a troubled ocean."

Clarence said, "Maybe General Grant got lucky. Like me." He folded the newspapers and pushed them toward me. "Save 'em for the next generation. Maybe for your kid at Columbia. I went there, too, after arriving back on July 3 from Brest, France. Our officer of the deck said, 'You and Cohen,' who just happened to be a plumber from Somerville, 'have been selected to attend Columbia University.'

"We were very near the Columbia College campus and were driven there in a U.S. Navy car. But the very next day, college was interrupted when we were sent to Hoboken to load groceries on the Vaterland, a troopship, later named the Leviathan. Cohen called it the Levi Nathan." A cursed or blessed memory like a steel trap gripped Clarence.

"A few days later I was sent with John Philip Sousa's band to sell Liberty War Bonds at theaters in New York City. That was a cheap way to get into the burlesque shows, but after a few weeks I was dispatched again as a gunner on a ship captured from Germany, called the Prinz Sigismund, that was loaded with ammunitions to take to Bordeaux, France. When we got back to New York on New Years, the war was over, so Harry Warner hired me at $10.00 a day…plus my dinner…at the Biograph Studios in New York City. That's how I ended up as an extra in the movies. Can't remember if it was <u>My Four Years in Germany</u> or <u>Mutiny on the Bounty</u>."

Clarence's eyes were a pale blue and half closed, but his bushy eyebrows added life to the story as they moved together in a dynamic that augmented his words. He was humming along with his phantasmagorical tale and then dropped a cherry on the top. "Then the nearly unknown Bert Lahr wanted me to travel in his summer theater crew through New Hampshire. So that's all I got from my Ivy League education." And then, a toothy smile that told me it didn't matter. "Nothin.'"

The old man was remembering those days with some fondness when he quietly pulled from his pocket his beloved Bertha's silver thimble. She could sew aprons, dresses and curtains and she could tailor suits. She could mend, darn, and repair zippers. You had to be smart and clever to sew like Bertha.

While she may not have had her own teeth by the time she died, nor could she shake her cigarette addiction, beautiful Bertha with her fine skin and thick hair, her high cheekbones and obstructive pulmonary cough would live on in that tiny treasure cup of a thimble. This is how I remember her.

Now is decades later and I'm curious to understand how

Clarence knew I could be entrusted with the thimble and his grandfather's Civil War newspapers. Did he guess that I would drive all over Los Angeles looking for someone to restore and laminate those newspapers in order to save them? Did he imagine I'd display Bertha's thimble in my china cabinet? Was it intuition or a clue from something I may have said?

◁◉

Mother often spoke of handwriting on the wall in relation to the Holocaust, illness, or old age. I believe she meant the nearly imperceptible cues, the peripheral and fleeting visions she noted on the march toward decline that my father and Clarence recognized as inexorable. When I can bear to be unemotional about loss, I'm able to distinguish some faint though legible handwriting on my wall as I hear of classmates, neighbors, and family members who quit fighting and disappeared. Now and then I add numbers and write fractions like a bookkeeper and note how depleted our ranks have become from those born in my birth year. I am aware. So these days I take more seriously my task of sorting and designating. While much of my accumulation is just sentimental or plays into a nonsensical fear that I might "need it some day," I remain attached nonetheless. I confess I keep among my valuables my grandfather's fingernail clippers, inherited in 1953, my mother's favorite tattered sheet music of "Wedding of the Painted Dolls," and a brown ceramic garden frog that's too tacky to put on view.

Little by little I'm releasing my personal cache in orchestrated handoffs. I clear, filter and shred my stuff, laundering like an editor and occasionally pruning like a southern gardener smothered by

118

an explosion of kudzu. This year I've culled and shredded certain pages from my 1959 diary when I was 16 lest some future reader misinterpret words from the boy crazy adolescent that would sully my reputation and out me for the vacuous fool I was. I try to decide if there's any historical, genealogical, sociological or literary reason to save such a book that compulsively details my phone calls, my hours of study, my math grades, and even the pimple that kept me home from school in embarrassment. Does anyone need to know the score of the hockey games or with whom I danced at the sock hop? Will it benefit my great grandchildren to know that I studied Latin really hard but hated my English teacher whose spittle spritzed on me as she yelled at me to "project my voice" and who stopped me in the corridor to comment, "I didn't know you were Jewish." I know it's an unimportant diary with boring ideas, the personal counterpart to today's tweeting, but I cannot throw away my opus that describes me at the time, a dedicated though lonely kid who knew she was obnoxious and melodramatic but continued in spite of that knowledge to write to her Dear Diary. In empathy today, I am kind to her, knowing she was just searching for her place in an often hostile high school world.

This 55-year-old locked leather diary with all its secrets is but one piece of debris that I, myself, cannot bear to throw away. Someone else will have to toss it after I'm gone and with my permission.

My only comfort lies in the knowledge that I'm not alone in this cycle. Most people keep collections they label treasure, and the converse is also true since beauty is in the eye of the beholder.

An obsidian pebble, a protective green stick from kindergarten, a photo that is thought to be a great grandmother because there's a resemblance in the smile. Or maybe it's a tiny silver thimble worn by a loved one or old newspapers that are the only remaining and easily portable remnants of a life. They are useless except for the relative nature of their value to their owners.

Some of the stuff gets pitched by its gatherer into the black hole of the dumpster after losing value to maturity, aging memories, or illness. Moves and forced attic cleanouts further thin the stash of mementos. Occasionally they disappear in a house fire or are carelessly discarded after a death. I'm hopeful that there's time to bequeath my own stash as did my father, Asher, Clarence and Clarence's grandfather.

While the treasured velocipede is long gone, Clarence did entrust Bertha's thimble and the old newspapers to me, soon to belong to my children and grandchildren, who were born more than a century after Clarence. Had they known Clarence or my father, they would have learned that old people, behind those bushy brows and faded eyes, harbor magical stories in a lifetime that wasn't always enchanting. My stories and magical moments will be different from theirs, peppered certainly with the lingo of genomes, 3-D printers, and computers that show images of velocipides, define them and then translate all into every language. Clarence who dabbled in the dream and hope of Esperanto, a common language for the people of the world that was to foster inclusivity and communication, never imagined the power of Google and the Cloud of this new world.

Grounding and securing me for now in this world are some

old newspapers, apothecary scales, a tiny thimble, a piece of sheet music, a brown pottery frog, nail clippers, and a fraternity pin. These artifacts keep alive the human cycle of treasuring, saving, and divesting which is as old as the hills. Sadly or happily for my progeny, I'm in the throes of adding my own contributions to the mix and starting to worry about who will become the anointed caretakers.

Freda A. Cohen, Palestine, 1922

Elixir for Auntie

The pregnant woman in the mirror with the enormous belly and those spindly legs had to give birth to that child... or die. I stared at my image and launched into a reality peptalk. "You are hardly the first woman to give birth. Other women have accomplished this and so can you." As I tiptoed toward the truth of my situation and stopped fighting, I believed I would achieve the status of an adult. I yearned for the relief of serenity that would follow acceptance when I could look in the mirror again without fear.

Sneaking back into my thinking was, "But you, in particular, have a low threshold for pain and it's obvious this baby is especially large. Why, even the itch of a mosquito bite drives you to distraction."

My interior monologue continued, "Now's the time to suck it up and stop trying to control everything. Just let it happen. The doctor is simply going to catch this baby and perhaps you'll get lucky like your friends, Sarah and Kate. "Pressure without pain." I repeated the mantra. "Pressure without pain."

Another image, this one from <u>Gone with the Wind</u>, superimposed itself, enhanced in Photoshop Technicolor. Melanie is stoic...but hemorrhaging nonetheless. She's dying in childbirth, saintly perhaps, but dead. I began bargaining or was it begging? If I can just get this over with soon, I can stop worrying. Knowing that terrible things do happen, even in the modern world, I didn't want the euphemistic label, "negative outcome" applied to me.

I needn't have carried on with such drama. While the blessed event occurred in a less auspicious manner than I'd planned, accompanied by an amniotic soaking of our only car, I was fine. The baby, while more nearly perfect than any other baby ever, was willful and determined to teach us the true meaning of exhaustion. Mine was the numbing kind of tired that knocks one off while sitting up or eating and where the mouth forms the O of near death. But more upsetting than the fatigue was that I, an honor student of Stone and Church, of Spock and Ginott, was unable to comfort my crying baby. More formula, different formula, booties on the feet or paregoric drops were useless. I wept, she screamed and my husband, the father, walked and walked in an attempt to comfort both of us.

Being the parent of this child turned out to be more complicated than taking my comprehensive exams in college, more terrifying than flying cross country to reunite with my fiancé in an airplane dripping god-knows-what on me, and far more wrenching than telling my mother, descended from 17 generations of rabbis, that I was determined to marry Ralph Malcolm Warrington, the 3rd.

It was in this chaotic setting that I accepted the deaths of my chronically sick paternal grandmother, Bubbie Haia, and also my mother's father, Alter. While I'd known them both well and visited weekly until I left for college, their passings were not particularly hard on me. My Bubbie Haia had lost her inhibitions and would spit out her pills beside the bed, and I knew that happened because she was very old. And my grandfather's cancer had spread to a hopeless degree. While unpleasant and sad for my parents, I was resigned to letting them go. In my infinite naïveté I understood I had no other option.

⊀©

This is the sum total of everything I knew about life and death until 10 years later when my great Auntie Freda was ailing. Ailing was her word, not mine, just as galoshes, valise and dearie were part of her personal lexicon. She was the wonder of my life, stepping in for her older sister, Mollie, my other grandmother, at all times and whenever I needed her. Born on January 12, 1901, she was no spring chicken when she enlisted in the U. S. Army as a nurse and then tramped muddy roads and soggy fields and kept the surgical tents as organized as possible during the Battle of the Bulge in World War II. Back home in New York City, she led a Spartan and cautious life, sometimes riding the D train to work at the Montefiore Hospital and sometimes walking. She counted and recounted her surgical instruments, autoclaved them to perfect sterilization, and received a gold watch after 25 years. If Auntie had a bit of chocolate peppermint patty, her favorite candy, she drank her tea without sugar. She exercised every morning, rolling back on her shoulders and bicycling with her feet in the air. For one small deviation from this normal discipline she was rewarded with a rug burn on her forehead at the age of 70 from a header into the carpet from our kids' slide.

❦

My Great Auntie Freda couldn't get a proper diagnosis for what was troubling her. One doctor in Florida used the C word and she felt doomed. I blathered to her a cascade of denials. "Don't talk that way, Auntie. (Refuse to name it.) Whatever it is we can beat it. (Live in an imaginary world order.) Keep your spirits up (With death nipping at your heels?) Think positive thoughts. (The lesions in my lungs will shrink)." With my head in the sand, I was denying the pain of a real discussion. It was the standard hedge against that shadow of imminence that hovers when time is short.

Our family flew Auntie from her tiny condo in Florida to the Taj Mahal of hospitals in Boston. It was the dead of winter and I'd come home to be nearby when Auntie was opened up and her lungs ransacked on a hunt for what appeared to be the metastatic lesions seen in her scans. Nothing pathological was found and we were filled with joy. Auntie recovered from the mining of her lungs by the best thoracic surgeons in the world and went home to Florida. She gave up on her plan to put her head in the oven.

When it was obvious that the doctors had missed something serious and Auntie was fading, I flew to Miami Beach to help her carry out her deathbed preparations and to get her situated in a proper care facility. I wrote checks for her with sadness and took her one ring out of the safe deposit box and accepted it as her final goodbye.

The nurses were very fond of Auntie and kindly assured me

they had a plan to mix her a Brompton's cocktail when the time came. The elixir was made of whiskey, morphine and cocaine, a throwback to the nineteenth century and named after a hospital in England. I'm suspicious, although the right word is proud, that Auntie, foresighted and innovative, handed her nurse friends the recipe when she was transferred to their facility for her end of life care. She'd spent plenty of time bivouacked in English pastures where she likely learned the intricacies of the lethal recipe from her colleagues. After dark there were no campfires allowed that might guide the German Luftwafte to their secret location. Instead the nurses had somber discussions about where they might be deployed, how to get some word past the censors and to their families, and how some of them in the 114th knew a humanitarian way to ease the most cruelly wounded into a compassionate passing. Not that they'd ever consider mixing up a Brompton's cocktail unless they considered the vow to "do no harm" be interpreted broadly to mean that there were times a sweetened few ounces of brandy with some additives would do less harm in extreme cases where there was no hope.

◖◉

During my week in Miami Beach I no longer felt hope and wasn't thinking like an adult when I hadn't a single helpful thought. I ran to her bank, wrote and mailed her checks, and asked for help from the nurse's station. I asked for a straw, some ice or an injection for pain. Auntie was unable to muster a smile at my carefully selected photos of her great grand nieces and nephew whom she adored. Chitchat was not fun for me and surely not possible for Auntie. What I witnessed was the certainty of her imminent death, not at all part of my plan for Auntie who was just supposed to go to sleep, gently and swiftly, and most of all, without suffering. And most certainly this misery could not have been God's plan for a patriot and the perfect great auntie.

My thoughts were fragmented and my nights long and interrupted by bad dreams. I was relieved to be staying at Auntie's neighbor Ann Matyck's apartment where I would not be alone with my racing thoughts. I was no longer in denial and knew my dear auntie's life would end today or tomorrow or the next day. I had to go home to my children, so I arranged her tissues and call button on the rolling table by her bed, put her slippers close by the bed in case by some miracle she was able to stand up. I kissed her goodbye. We both knew it was a final goodbye as we tried not to cry. We faked it, you might say. "Chin up, Dearie," were her final words to me before she fell into a blessed sleep.[1]

⊷

Ann Matyck drove me through a violent thunderstorm to the airport where I caught my flight back to Houston and my picture perfect family and life in the suburbs. While the airplane dipped and twisted in the vicious storm, I let go the grief of the week as I fought down nausea along with panic that I might never see my children again.

The next day, safe in my yellow kitchen with its harvest gold appliances, I was devastated to learn that Ann Matyck had

---

[1] Auntie Freda A. Cohen would be pleased to know that she's buried in plot 34 0 593 at Barrancas National Cemetery just an arrow shot away from the beautiful Ha-ga, wife of Geronimo who is close by in grave #1496. She and Auntie had a lot in common with their dedication to their missions and the people they loved. I'm comforted in the hope that their spirits can hang out together.

stepped out of her car into a deep puddle and was electrocuted by a live wire that had fallen into the street. And the following week, Auntie died from metastatic something. No one in our family by then cared where the primary tumor had been hiding and we refused an autopsy.

Today, as I reflect on the last few months of Auntie's life, I suspect that those wonderful doctors from the Taj Mahal of hospitals who probed, snipped and studied the slides both in the operating room and later in the pathology lab, made a decision they believed was best for all of us. I believe they took a bow and played God. As peppered with dangerous lesions as she was, it made no sense to let her, or our family, know of the futility of the rest of her days. Might they have hoped she would have a few happy weeks or months without the anxiety of knowing the end was upon her so soon? Medical mores don't stand still although we might like to believe that the ethics remain constant, with right being right and wrong being wrong and absolutely so. While honesty has been my mantra, I think that if what I now believe did transpire, I owe a debt of gratitude for the good doctors' decision.

Dying as a Complication of Living

Orchestration and planning is a good thing when it comes to Classical music. Without those attributes, it's said to be noise, like trashcans banging and random car horns honking. The composer has a plan, listens carefully, hears his vision, creates balance and maybe harmony among his instruments, and tries to pull together the entire work to make musical sense both for the musician and the listener. If the composer did otherwise, the orchestra would sound like the hatik tsuris my mother accused us kids of creating in our living room. She used "tsuris," a perfect Yiddish word meaning "trouble" or "aggravation," to describe the pain of listening to our piano mistakes.

By the time we were old enough to begin music lessons, Mother had lost her own mother to tuberculosis. She'd suffered the loss of her father's family in the Holocaust, had nearly died in childbirth, and survived one bloody miscarriage. Hers had not been an easy life and she believed that keeping order was the only way she knew to get through law school while visiting her mother in a sanitorium twice a week, cooking and cleaning for her younger brother and father, and taking over as the buyer at the family's dress shop. She obsessed over her detailed plans and followed them through to completion as best she could. She weighed and measured everything against everything else: to ride the trolley or to save the nickel for a cucumber sandwich; to bake flounder or fry up mackerel for her father and brother; to take the bus on Shabbos to see her mother in the hospital or to try to get special permission from the hospital to visit on another day.

Mother was meticulous about her life and that's why she could correctly assess her bids and remember exactly how many and which spades were out in her bridge games. Her orderly brain functioned so clearly that she passed the Massachusetts State Bar Exam when she was barely 21 years old.

Along with a village of others from the Old Country, New York and Palestine, Mother had great respect for her grandfather, Rabbi Baruch Cohen, known for his interpretation of dreams and his high ethical standards. Perhaps his suggestion that she lay her study papers under her pillow the night before the exam had something to do with her success.

Mother's obsessive mind drove us, her four children, mad with her Bible-like notebooks of details and her financial ledgers accounting for every stock split and dividend to the penny. We begged her to focus some of her attention on an entertaining book or television show to deflect her intolerable anxiety level when she had tax estimates to prepare or a check to write.

All to no avail. And in step with her need to keep her life in perfect order, Mother attempted to orchestrate her own passing in order to make it "easy" for us children. She signed her health care proxy, understood it completely, and even drafted similar documents for elderly friends as she preached the importance of creating such a legal document. We, her four adult children, never could have envisioned what was to happen.

With caution and sorrow in her black eyes that were nearly blind from cataracts, she listened to her excellent geriatrician ask the Do Not Resuscitate question. I was on the telephone extension at the recommendation of the doctor and Mother, at 93, listened closely and decided to consult with her trusted youngest son, my brother the computer scientist, before she gave her answer. "Do you think it's the right thing to do?" Mother asked him. And with tears in his eyes he answered slowly but simply in the affirmative.

Outside the window of Mother's corner apartment on the 12th floor was a great view of the George Washington Bridge that was especially pretty at night as lights outline its graceful form. But inside her apartment as her door closed, one could clearly see taped to the back of the door the DNR orders for anyone who might attempt to go against her wishes. The placement may sound cruel, but my mother was bent nearly to the floor and could not see the back of the door without a lot of effort. The DNR was meant for any bold ambulance driver who might try to drag my mother kicking and screaming to the closest contracted hospital and start hooking her up to unwanted heroic measures, if she were to fall. One night she did slip off her bed and pulled a pillow down to spend the night on the floor so as not to disturb my brother to come until morning. My mother was always thoughtful. She was also very stubborn and refused to let me put away the dangerously slippery silk comforter that was a wedding gift from her mother-in-law 71 years earlier. It was most certainly her comfort comforter.

In my mind, the independent living facility, always fearful of a lawsuit, conspired willfully to deny Mother her wishes for refusing heroic measures. It was a win–win for no one. If a resident calls for help from the floor, standard protocol is an automatic call to the ambulance. The ambulance could pick up a resident from the floor and assess for damage, but the facility wants to protect itself and its residents by taking everyone immediately to the hospital after even the gentlest of slips or slides.

Our family, with its financial resources, love, and scientific knowledge, joined this conspiracy and participated in a loving cycle we helped create to jam Mother's plans. It was a gentle version of hell in the name of the best quality of in-home care we could find as we attempted to Lock Mother Into Life. We had the finest medical team consisting of a Harvard Medical School trained geriatrician, her nurse practitioner, a cardiologist, a weight nurse to monitor daily fluid retention and a slew of hospice personnel from the director, to the social worker, case nurse and aides who came 20 to 40 hours a week to augment and direct our loving private duty aides.

My mother always told me she just wanted to go to sleep and not wake up. How far off we migrated from her orchestrated plan to slip quietly into the shadows. Along with her specific instructions that we not mourn for her but think kindly instead, she insisted that she'd had a good life and her children, grandchildren and great grandchildren were wonderful. In fact, she was convinced they were perfect.

We were naïve to believe that, with the requisite paperwork in place, mother would find an easy peace as she drifted into the next world, whenever and wherever that might be. The reality, however, stinks. There was no plug to pull even if one of us had the will or courage to pull it. The carefully chosen caregivers "got food into her" as if she were a baby bird who prematurely fluttered out of her nest. Every time she opened her eyes, someone yelled, "Open your mouth, please, Mrs. S." Dutifully, though with eyes closed and head lolling off to one side, Mother opened her mouth just enough for her caregivers to slip in some nourishment. Sometimes they tapped her mouth with a straw and she was thirsty enough to suck up an energy drink or ginger ale.

And there was one miraculous day when mother awoke to remind us that she was still in this world. "Don't shout," she said and shattered our rationalizations which went like this: Mother can't hear what we're saying because Mother is in a fog and Mother cannot feel anything much. The next day her caregiver accidentally hit her in the nose while reaching across her bed. Mother woke up and said, "No punching in the nose." Everyone had a good laugh.

Mother's occasional drift back to our world was an uneasy reminder that, while we wished for Mother to slide gently to death, she was still here. We four children lost our collective nerve and went with the flow of caregivers who were trying to keep her alive and we (shame on us) wondered if they were just saving their jobs. We could not stop feeding Mother because she was able to swallow and to chew a little. We could not stop lifting her to the commode because she did not want to soil herself and had perfect control. And through it all, we attempted to catch her between semi-lucid moments with one or both eyes open.

◖

I sing and entreat Mother to try to "Twinkle Twinkle Little Star" with me in the hope that, if it is a stroke that takes away her ability to speak, the automatic singing spot in her brain will release her normal speech. We are not asking much when we hope for her to give us a sign that she knows us. When her eyes are open, she squeezes her caregiver's hand. Don't leave me. Is that what she is saying? I'm so afraid so hold onto me? And I, her daughter, now elderly and living in another state, have come to watch the heartbreaking drama only to leave without even a smile of recognition. And all the while, I believe in the depths of my guilty heart that I should be at the bedside holding Mother's hand in a deathwatch. And since that does not appear imminent, unfortunately, that leads to self-loathing for my selfish bad attitude. But then I have the conversation with myself about Mother's loss of dignity, of control, of our personal pain in seeing our formerly beautiful and strong Mother heaped onto her commode in the nude so as not to soil her clothes. Won't it be better if Mother will simply spit out the food and quit eating? We will respect her wishes. And what decision do we make about the morphine for her torn up knee because now she's paranoid and hallucinating from the medications?

And then I slam myself...who do I think I am? God? For heaven's sake. What is my problem with control? With letting go our grand plan, hers and ours? Life and death is not up to me, now, is it? And the inner dialogue continues day in and day out without my being able to shut down my circle of helplessness.

My friends have all been through this end of life suffering with one or both parents and offer me great support. They speak of the dignity we have given Mother by providing outstanding care. They don't blame me for not loitering in the shadows every day waiting for her to open her eyes. They know me well enough to know my huge tolerance for psychic pain that has played out over my lifetime, but this time I cannot and am not the good daughter for my mother's final journey. I am incapable of doing anything now except hoping for an end to this limboland for mother and for us four adult children.

I have learned that there is no art, science, or plan that is useful when it comes to dying, though we all are duped into feeble attempts to get a handle on the process in case we get lucky and the DNR papers do their job. We buy extra coverage for care insurance to lure us into complacency thinking that, with enough help, we'll be clean and fed until we drift off. We situate ourselves in a daughter's guest room, or a made-over garage, or an assisted living facility with levels of care. And then we often wait too long to stop breathing because all this great care keeps us barely here and mostly there. Look at my beautiful and dear Mother who is propped up in a chair now with an ulcer beginning on her leg, cheyne stoking because of her two faulty valves, in her Depends undergarment. Her clever black eyes are closed. Nurses and aides and family are coming and going. An old friend from her table downstairs, wide-eyed and silent, awaiting her turn, sits patiently by Mother's side.

One cannot lay an ounce of blame on Mother when it's evident that her heart is giving out. She did exercise; she did not eat meat; she did not have diabetes. Her heart gave out in spite of her walking the hills, jumping red hot pepper into her 50s and never touching a hamburger. It happened because she was lucky enough to get very old.

When my mother smiles at her caregivers during a bed bath, as they wash her inside and out, I wonder if she enjoys all this attention. Never before has anyone taken care of her, putting a straw to her lips and blending her food or cutting it up so that she can chew little pieces of her fruit salad which she loves so much. Maybe, I should lighten up and reframe my attitudes and feelings to reflect the possibility that Mother is having the best time of her life. No paperwork or numbers to work, no hearing aid batteries to install, no logistics of getting drivers or her sons to take off from work to take her to a doctor appointment, no aggravation about the $6,000 bridge falling out of her mouth once a month, no dragging her weak body all the way to the dining room, no need to argue with me every day about allowing us to buy her a new TV or recliner or wheelchair, no birthday or holiday cards to write, or gift checks, or return calls or cataract decisions.

Life now is simple for Mother with no more decisions. Except one. To eat or not to eat? That is Mother's only choice.

Mother stopped eating on November 27 and died on the afternoon of November 29, 2009 at the age of 93. The sun streamed into her west facing bedroom and bathed her dead body in a beautiful glow as befitted my mother. Shortly afterward my brother took down the DNR sign from her door.

Bought With Butter

The Story of the Burkett Clock

The tall-case clock was bought and paid for with butter in 1805 by the second **John Burkit (Feb. 22, 1773 – Nov 26, 1859)** of Kingwood Township, Hunterdon County, New Jersey. John was married on Mar 18, 1809 to Mary Fox (Nov 1, 1783 – May 21, 1838). They had ten children (Charles, Rachel, George W., Jackson, C., Elizabeth, Mary, Silvester H., Amy, John, and Keziah).

The clock was sold at John Burkit's estate sale and bought by his son, **Charles Burkett (Oct. 27, 1810 – Nov 4, 1887),** for seven dollars in December of 1859. Charles was married on Nov. 2, 1833 to Nancy Housel (May 17, 1815 – July 14, 1902). Their children were Thomas P., Mary Elizabeth, Delilah C., and Charles Stout Burkett.

Charles Stout Burkett, (August 23, 1849 – April 5, 1914) married Emma Jane Cawley (Jennie) (1851 – December16, 1935) on May 10, 1871. Charles S. bought the clock at his father's estate sale in 1898 for $175.

Charles Stout willed the clock to his son, Franklin Earle Burkett (Earle) around 1915. **Franklin Earle Burkett (Nov. 25, 1882 – December 7th, 1951)** married Ethel Rae Reichard (Jan. 1, 1888 – February 7, 1967) on May 5, 1909. Their children were Ruth Anna, Charles Franklin, and Dorothy Ethel Burkett.

When Franklin Earle died the clock was willed to his son, **Charles Franklin Burkett (Feb. 14, 1914 – October 11, 1994)** who kept it until he died. After his death, his widow, Jeanne Schoenbaum Burkett (October 22, 1910 – October 20, 2002), kept the clock until her death. Charles and Jeanne were married on September 25, 1937.

Jeanne Schoenbaum Burkett's niece, **Phyllis Schoenbaum Lange**, executrix of her aunt's estate, contacted the clock's rightful owner, the eldest son in the Burkett line, **Ralph Malcolm Warrington, III**. He has now assumed responsibility as the current keeper of the Burkett tall-case clock. The first owner,

John Burkit was Ralph Malcolm Warrington, III's great-great-great grandfather.

The Author Gratefully Acknowledges the Contributions to this story by:

- Dr. David Sperling, tall-case clock expert, who has been most generous with his time,
- Sue Roecker, cousin, serendipitously located while researching the clock's history,
- Phyllis Schoenbaum Lange, executrix of the Charles F. and Jeanne Burkett estate.

The story of how this tall-case clock came to rest in the home of the great-great-great grandson of its first owner, John Burkit of Kingwood, Hunterdon County, New Jersey has turned upside down my nearly complete acceptance of the belief that stuff shouldn't matter too much in the grand scheme. I've struggled for years to overcome my pride in ownership of beautiful things and I'd embraced the idea that detachment from worldly artifacts would motivate me toward a more positive and grateful outlook on life. However, the Burkit tall-case clock in our foyer is a reminder that Buddhist-style ascetic simplicity is not for me. I admit to being sufficiently proud of its ownership by my husband that I've given up all hope of divestment and have become unashamedly reattached to my favorite stuff.

As the admitted prideful owner of family artifacts that provide comfort and a sense of my own family history, ties to the past, and a general historical perspective, I was dismayed to discover that my husband had no such feelings toward any object or relative more distant than a sibling. In fact, he wasn't comfortably familiar with the kinship vocabulary of "aunt," "first cousin once removed" or "great uncle." These words were as foreign to him as if he'd sprung from some unique tribal society in the Amazon, not because his relatives didn't exist somewhere, but because there was no connection.

The first mention of this grand clock happened 50 years ago when we were newlyweds. It happened just before my young husband, with the gusto of youth, shook a loose-lidded Ketchup bottle and splattered my yellow pants and sweater in a most ghoulish pattern. My mother-in-law had just been warning us that we mustn't let the clock disappear, because her brother, the current keeper of the clock, had no heirs. She was undoubtedly thinking about the old clock she'd grown up with as she scrubbed away the red stains from my inappropriate-for-the-Maine-woods yellow outfit.

My mother-in-law died young but I never forgot her warning about losing the clock to strangers who would care nothing about its history. Her brother, my husband's uncle, died many years later at a reasonably old age. Except for what he'd left to the church, his wife Jeanne had inherited everything, including the clock. We discovered later that the will did not assign the clock upon her death to my husband, the third Ralph Malcolm Warrington, the man who did not know an uncle from a first cousin once removed. Rather, it was by word of mouth that the estate's attorney made clear, as did the executrix of her will, that the clock belonged to Charles' first nephew, my husband.

To be honest, I cared more about the clock than my husband

did, for I saw its presence in our home as a teaching opportunity. He had no clear sense of where he fit into his family with its long and documented history. This clock presented the best opportunity to connect with a past, his past.

◖◗

I understood exactly how I fit into my own fearful Jewish family who experienced a rampant anti-Semitism that translated to potentially being annihilated at any moment. Therefore, it's with precision that I can locate myself on our family trees.

I knew the old folks on both sides of my family, people who had either survived pogroms or the Holocaust or had serendipitously gotten ahead of it in the great migrations to America from Russia, Poland, and Lithuania. Our family kept in touch with or knew who landed in the new diaspora of Canada, South America, South Africa, and Mexico. These old folks pinched my cheeks and patted my hands. They sewed me skirts with eyelet ruffles and baked me strudel and called me *shana madel*. I have their old postcards among my late grandmother's and mother's photos.

I began to own that history as I polished for years the squat brass samovar and tray I inherited from my mother. The contraption with its eight pieces was a fixture on my grandmother's mantel and then my mother's mantel and finally in my living room, although I'd never seen live coals glowing in its chimney. This brass samovar was my mother's prized possession as it had been passed along to her from previous generations from Briansk, Poland until it landed in America. The hot samovar tea, sipped through a sugar cube held between the front teeth, was served to many an old rabbi in the old country who stopped by to discuss relevant ethical issues and practical considerations such as what to do about the devastating fire in the family's brewery. Now the samovar has become a valuable reminder of the past.

Among my inherited treasures is a brass tray table and its folding legs carried from Palestine to America in 1932 on an ocean liner and under the arm of my great auntie Freda. What kind of a message did she bring to the family, I always wondered. The Hebrew inscription on the table reads, "If I forget you O Israel, may my tongue stick to the roof of my mouth." I've interpreted it in my own way and am grateful for air-conditioning and unlimited drinking water from a municipal system.

Even my father's giant mortar and pestle from the back room of his former drugstore command my respect along with his pharmacopeia of medicinal recipes and his eyecup since one never knows exactly when one might need to rinse out an irritant. Then, there's my mother's cereal bowls, the first melamine dishes, produced about 1938. I can see her Sunday school class wrapping them in newspaper for her wedding shower gift and hopping with delight at my mother's exuberant thank you's.

The list of my family treasures is unlimited and they exist for me not as clutter but as context. They place me in the world and within a family, not exactly warm and fuzzy, but comforting nonetheless.

Still, I knew I needed to downsize and address my packrat tendencies while deemphasizing connections to worldly goods. I was making progress at least on the idea, the goal, of detachment until the Burkit (Burkett) clock surfaced.

FIRST GENERATION
John Burkit
February 22, 1773 – November 26, 1859

In the mid-1700s the John Burkit family owned a dairy farm whose property abutted George Fox's in Kingwood Township, Hunterdon County, New Jersey. The County always hired meticulous surveyors to measure property with the Fox/Burkit stone mentioned in deeds of transference at one common corner. With 32 chains and 20 links on one side together with three other measurements, the Burkit tract amounted to 102 acres "more or less," along with 122 birch trees that grew on the property.

Checking on the condition of the Burkit birches and the chestnut wormwood fences gave John's son, young John, a good excuse to go to the back of his property to meet George's daughter, Mary, at "their" designated stone. This stone, more a small boulder to lean upon than a flat rock for sitting, became the site for clandestine meetings for the young John and Mary, George's daughter. After laughing about the sermon, or Mrs. Rittenhouse's outlandish hat, or the deep mud in front of the church where Mrs. Stout slipped and fell, or just about any old thing, John would concoct an excuse to traipse into the back field to meet Mary and touch her shoulder or her sackcloth skirts. And then came the guilty kiss with John wanting more and Mary thinking of matrimony without considering the possibility that God would send her 10 children. The following Sunday John would venture out to the Flemington Presbyterian Church on

Main Street and occasionally have the pleasure of collecting Mary and her mother in the Burkit horse and buggy. The young people would sneak a message setting the time for their next rendezvous. So their rock in the field became a third party to the process of courtship, a solid metaphor for their sacred union yet to come.

After each assignation Mary's father, George, quizzed her as he noticed the stickers on her long skirts and stockings. Mary had an easy answer since there was always some chore or lost cow drunk on Jimson weed to be tended to toward the back of the hayfields.

In the meantime John had taken to crossing Main Street from the Presbyterian Church in Flemington to Hooley's Place at #46 where Richard Hooley from Massachusetts had set up a fine shop in 1796. John admired the clocks and jewelry in the shop and more than anything, except for Mary, he wanted a tall-case clock just like the one in the shop.

John negotiated a deal to pay for a clock with fancy Chippendale hands and a beautiful painted dial from Boston's Curtis and Nolen. The men shook hands as John promised Mr. Hooley at least three pounds of butter a week seemingly until the end of time. Since Burkit's butter was said to be every bit as good and soft as the Capner's butter bought by Martha Washington and sent along for George with his wooden teeth,[1] Hooley believed he had negotiated the better deal.

Once the new tall-case clock was completed in Flemington, delivered, and set in the great room of the farmhouse in 1805, its

[1]The nation's capitol was in Philadelphia for 10 years while the Washington capitol was being constructed.

brass finials reaching to nearly eight feet, young John wondered if its presence in his home would tempt his neighbor, Mary, into accepting his proposal of marriage. John did impress her father, George Fox, who asked him to wait for Mary a few more years. John, being 10 years older than Mary, knew how to charm a woman and finally proposed, leaning against their rock when Mary was 26 years old and beginning to think of herself as a spinster. They were happily married in late winter of 1809 and soon forgot about their rock.

The Foxes and the Burkits had their share of disagreements over the Baptists versus the Methodists versus the Presbyterians versus the Lutherans. There was always some scandal to discuss or, more pressing, the benefits of lime versus manure. John believed that spreading manure was like constructing rock walls...too labor-intensive. The manure chore was tedious and, not to mention in front of the ladies, pungent. Lime was the better way to restore fertility to the earth. Yes, 50 to 100 bushels of slacked lime per acre.

The converse belief belonged to Mr. Fox who was certain that good old manure was tried and true. Young John scoffed and laughingly noted the invasive weeds and saplings that sprouted from manure. Mr. Fox had no response except to personalize the conversation by suggesting that young John was a little on the lazy side, like the rest of his generation. That was when John asked his father-in-law if he thought Robert Fulton was lazy when he patented and built his steamboat. Mr. Fox replied that he would not be caught dead on that ocean voyage from New York Harbor to Philadelphia on a boat with a giant wheel.

They backed each other into corners of arguments but

enjoyed the sparring enough to continue. Whether manure or lime won the debate, Mary didn't care. She was adamant about one thing: a farmer's clothes must dry out in the barn before he might enter the house and then only through the kitchen door.

After a long day of milking, haying, tilling, sharpening, or repairing, John often sat by the evening fire with his eyes closed and listened to the steady sounds of his clock. The serious question in Mary's mind was whether he loved her or his clock more. He took great satisfaction in its precision time keeping and felt a measure of pride that its inner workings were made up the road in Northern West New Jersey in Hunterdon County. Each part was perfectly machined and tooled. The winding drums were made of thin and smoothly rolled brass. The Federal Hepplewhite mahogany case and the broken arch pediment may have been copied from Richard Hooley's colleagues in Flemington, but they were simpler in that the ends weren't decorated. That fit just right in John's simple farmhouse although the three brass finials atop the short chimneys projected elegance geared more for the likes of General and Mrs. George Washington. As for those hemispheric maps below the moon dial...they reminded John that there existed oceans and lands far beyond his 102 acres.

This particular clock melded the function of perfect timekeeping and the beauty of a case with oval burled crotch wood inlays and an exquisitely painted moon dial. While his Christian instincts condemned pride of ownership of worldly goods, John was not ashamed. This tall clock could have graced the palace of the King of England.

When they married, Mary was not thinking about 10 children in that household, 10 children who had to behave with decorum enough not to dent the mahogany case or break the glass in front of the painted iron dial. She allowed no roughhousing to knock the pendulum out of alignment, no dirty boots to scar the ovals in the shield-shaped door, and no leaning against the quarter columns on either side of the clock.

Mr. Hooley's clock now belonged to the Burkits and its chiming and steady rhythms comforted both Mary and John through difficult times. Those Burkit babies, after all, did not sprout up like beans from Mary's womb. And although death threatened time after time to conquer by taking one or another of the children, and finally did overtake George W., young John, and Rachel before their 40th birthdays, most of the family survived. John believed the clock watched over them with more benevolence than the God of their church who was convinced they were sinners and in need of some serious redemption. In fact, John refused to allow Mary to call upon the doctors in Flemington, even those graduates from the University of Pennsylvania School of Medicine. With all their modern training, they drained their patients' blood with leeches, forced them to swallow runaway mercury, and blistered them up with mustard poultices. John was convinced those do-no-harm doctors were as ruthless as the judges in Salem who hanged witches at Gallows Hill.

On March 24, 1825 when John and Mary were married 17 years and had added eight children to the family, mostly without the help of a doctor, the first issues of the <u>Hunterdon Gazette</u>

and <u>Farmers Weekly Advertiser</u> were published. Suddenly the Burkit's world expanded well past Kingwood and Frenchtown to the far reaches of Hunterdon County and beyond. The precious old editions were neatly stacked for future reference or for reading practice and were preferred by the children to <u>The New England Primer</u>, a chore after the first dozen readings and recitations. The <u>Primer</u> content spawned arguments over whether the D verse, the B verse or the W verse was more fun to read. Arguments were earnest but useless. Did the Deluge, or The Book, or Washington chapter offer up more excitement, inspiration, and historical interest? The children ganged up with their small army of agreeable siblings and mostly refused to accept arbitration by any higher authority. That persistence, or character flaw of obstinacy perhaps bred of necessity, served the Burkit family well and into the future.

The <u>Gazette's</u> publication provided the impetus for the townspeople to come together to plan a proper Fourth of July celebration for the summer of 1825. It was in the Kingwood Tavern, the same place that sheltered travelers in 1764 on the Kings Highway and served as a recruitment location for men ready to join the Hunterdon County Militia, that men met to plan the summer's Independence Day celebration. The glorious party was to begin with a 50-gun salute at sunrise and then a procession of 42 Revolutionary War veterans, including two black veterans. They were to march from General Price's house on the corner of Mine and Main Street and then past John and Mary's Presbyterian Church. Each veteran would receive a white ribbon badge with an American eagle stamped on it along with the words, "Survivors of 1776."

With the three taverns in full view along Main Street, John was reminded of the story of Paul Revere's gallop 50 years earlier in April of 1775 just two years after he was born. John wondered if he would ever make as great a contribution to the country as Revere and Dawes had made when, as a members of the Sons of Liberty, they saw those two lanterns shining for 60 seconds in the belfry of the North Church. How they managed to sneak a boat ride across the Charles River with all those Redcoats swarming over Boston as well as all the curfews in place was simple good luck. Their ride over land once they crossed the Charles became a mad dash to Lexington in order to warn Adams and Hancock that the British were on their way to Concord and the munitions stash.

It was sheer irony that Revere's luck changed when he was captured in a field and his horse stolen after he successfully made enough noise to wake the dead outside the house where Adams and Hancock were staying. When telling his children the story, John always told them the war was won because the British were slow and took their good old time, enjoying taverns along the road. The moral to the story was to stay out of those taverns although that was where Revere and his friend, William Dawes, had overheard the British chatter that spoke of plans to arrest Adams and Hancock and get to the much needed munitions.

There is a time and place for a visit to Smick's Tavern, thought John Burkit, but today was not the day. He had chores to do on the farm, butter to churn, moldy hay to clear out of the barn, and lime to rake in and under. While Charles, Rachel, George and Jackson ranged in ages from 15 to nine years old, John knew they couldn't do much without the specific directions of what, where, and how. As for the little children, they were only helpful to Mary to mind themselves and each other.

And poor Mary? She was expecting again and not happy with John, for she'd figured out long ago that her babies were not God's will alone. For those reasons and more, John knew he'd better not stop at Smick's but head straight home as soon as the procession ended.

Although Mary was a strong woman, she died shortly after her 55th birthday. She'd given birth every other year for 20 years and her last child, Keziah, was only nine years old when her mother died.

John lived another 21 years and likely stopped by their rock now and then to remember happier times.

SECOND GENERATION
Charles Burkett
October 27, 1810 - November 4, 1887

Charles was 49 years old when his father, John, died. As expected, Charles, as the firstborn son, was given the opportunity to buy the Hooley tall-case clock at his father's estate sale in December of 1859. He paid seven dollars for the clock that had been a dynamic part of his life since he was born.

Charles Burkett and his wife, Nancy Housel, had been married 26 years when they brought that clock to their home. Thomas,

Mary Elizabeth, Delilah, and Charles Stout Burkett ranged in age from 23 down to 10 years old when it arrived. The big argument at that time between Nancy and Charles was whether to remove the brass finials on top or remove the skirting at the base of the clock so it would fit in the entryway to their house. The skirt was sacrificed.

The Hooley clock must have enjoyed quiet respite in Charles' and Nancy's care after its stay in John and Mary's household with its 10 children. Unlike her mother-in-law, Mary, God brought Nancy a more manageable four children. And those four children somehow survived to adulthood and had children of their own.

The members of the two Baptist churches in town were at war with each other and the old Baptist church had even voted to suspend the followers of the new church. Mr. Wigg, with his fancy salary of $250 a year, was the new pastor.

Charles and Nancy felt more blessed than not when their two daughters married the Rittenhouse brothers, Jeremiah and the Reverend Elisha, men of God, though Baptists. It was close to impossible for even the best of men and women to belong to that church even if they agreed to reach out to the Indians to bring them into the fold or even if the congregants could tolerate the long and tedious services. Charles and Nancy believed that many of those people who stood up during meetings were pontificating just to prove how dedicated they were to the American Particular Baptists' strict beliefs. They themselves watched and listened but were still uncertain about predestination and occasionally lapsed into private conversations about the futility of it all. Would they be asked to remain members or called upon to leave the Church due to questionable piety? In modern times it might be said that the Burketts kept a low profile while the church continued to be divisive and exclusive.

A conflict larger than the one at church was smoldering among the politicians and ordinary men of the northern and southern states. The unity of the new country was being threatened and Charles, like many others, understood the enormity of the issues. As a farmer he saw the need for help in the fields. And while he didn't own slaves or indentured help, he paid close attention to what his farmer friends said as well as Abraham Lincoln who was practically his twin in age. Charles respected him as a shrewd and strategic thinker whose ideas were all the talk in the towns' taverns. Charles, like Lincoln, agreed that owning another man would be as morally corrupt as owning his wife, Nancy, as if she were a productive cow or even a beautiful clock.

While New Jersey regiments were always looking to muster young men, Charles, 51 years old at the start of the Civil War, was too old to enlist. Although there was no conscription requirement at the time, he and Nancy worried instead about Thomas, their firstborn, who was eventually conscripted into the Union Army by the law of 1863. He'd be leaving his wife, Maggie and their two little ones, Martha and Minnie.

◖◗

Although Thomas did return home, he was mentally and physically scarred like most men who go to war. After the tragedy of the war between brothers in the North and the South, he was never the same. While he lived 20 years longer, he died less than two months after his father.

While his wife, Maggie, would have loved to keep the clock, she understood and accepted the tradition of patrimonial inheritance. She knew this clock was destined for Charles S., her brother-in-law, as the next male child of Charles and Nancy's four children.[2]

In the end Charles and Nancy joined most of the family in Frenchtown Cemetery, a place to rest in eternity that would feel like home.

THIRD GENERATION
Charles Stout Burkett
August 23, 1849 – April 5, 1914

The very first thing that Charles Stout Burkett and his wife, Jennie (Emma Jane Cawley) did after moving the clock to their home in Oxford, New Jersey[3] was to have four knobby little feet crafted of mahogany and then secured to the bottom where the tall clock's original skirt had been attached. It would keep the clock off the cold floor and would prevent dampness or mold from accumulating underneath, thereby setting the scene for rot.

Charles S. was coughing by the turn of the century but was told he had a simple catarrh and not to worry about anything

---

[2] The Burkett clock did not leave Nancy Housel Burkett's household, though, until the turn of the century after Nancy passed away.

[3] about 30 miles north of Kingwood Township

worse. Jennie liked to look for a reason that Charles was coughing and while probably not true, she blamed the cough on the great blizzard of 1888, known to some as the Great White Hurricane. In that storm, hundreds of people died from Baltimore to Maine. They drowned crossing the frozen East River in New York City and they were found frozen to death standing upright in snowdrifts on the way to their barns. Some people were electrocuted by downed wires in the cities. For Charles S., the stress of the storm and of keeping his wife and six- and eight-year-old children safe and warm for the next weeks, was enough, Jennie believed, to have given birth to this wretched cough. For a long time, Charles S. sipped Mrs. Winslow's Soothing Syrup, but then he switched to Dr. Seth Arnold's Cough Killer that was supposed to tackle the night sweats and fevers.

When his health didn't improve, the doctor finally prescribed opium drops. But Charles S. began to fear tuberculosis. While he'd heard of Thomas Edison's X-ray machine that could have confirmed the awful possibility, there was nothing to be done about tuberculosis except total bed rest and fresh air. So why would he subject himself to X-rays that could leave him dead? He knew also that a law had been passed (1912) that mandated doctors report cases of tuberculosis to the county health official. Charles S., formerly a very strong man, wasn't quite ready to admit to the world that he might be dying.

Tuberculosis turned out to be the correct diagnosis. Charles S. rested often hoping to be one of the few who recovered. He slept outdoors on the porch whenever possible, but he became weaker until he was considering a sanatorium, a place that terrified him since he believed it was where people went to await death.

By dying in the spring of 1914, just before Archduke Ferdinand of Austria was shot to death, Charles S. was spared the bloody details of the Great War, the senseless conflagration that killed and maimed millions among the younger generation, along with innocent civilians around the world.

Jenny shed her tears privately when her Charles slipped away from her and the family to became one of 4273 people that year to die in New Jersey from tuberculosis, the Great White Plague.

The week Charles S. died was the same week the churches in Kingwood in Frenchtown donated over $1,000 for their coal collection. In spite of all the damage done in the 19th century to the community by ostracizing people, by making judgments about whether they should stay or leave the church, parishioners united to support their needy neighbors. Everyone knew that while shoveling coal to stoke a fire was a boring and dirty process, freezing in one's home was not acceptable in a Christian community such as theirs.

FOURTH GENERATION
Franklin Earle Burkett

November 25, 1882 – December 7, 1951

It was May of 1911. Charles S. and Jenny were devastated at the loss of their first grandchild, Ruth, at 14 months of age. And, this first child of their son, Franklin Earle, adored her grandpa. But Charles S. knew in his heart of hearts that in spite of his great white handkerchief, he probably coughed all over this baby while bouncing her on his knee or crooning to her. "Meet me tonight in dreamland, by the light of the silv'ry moon…"[4]

Soon, she, too, had tuberculosis.

⟪◉

The fact that Charles S. wasn't certain he was cursed with tuberculosis at the time didn't make it any easier for him to accept responsibility and neither did the fact that Franklin and his wife, Ethel Rae (Reichard), never hinted in front of him or Jenny that the baby's death had anything to do with him. Still, it became his secret torment.

Baby Ruth's parents, Franklin Earle Burkett and Ethel Rae, didn't dare whisper the deadly word, tuberculosis, as though acknowledging it by name would give its existence credence and let out the secret from its bag of shame. Victims felt the stigma as though they were responsible for their own sickness through some personal frailty. The disease was in every corner of the country with sick people being transported to sanatoria located everywhere. New laws were passed to prohibit spitting in subways and on streets. Other laws required landlords to install windows in every room of their buildings and tenements, even if they senselessly opened up to another interior room. From cities to beaches to mountaintops and in suburbs, large sanatoria were springing up

---

[4] Lyrics for "Meet Me Tonight In Dreamland": Meet me tonight in dreamland under the silv'ry moon where love's sweet roses bloom. Come with the love light gleaming in your dear eyes of blue. Meet me in dreamland. Sweet dreamy dreamland, there let my dreams come true. (from the play In The Good Ol' Summertime, 1909)

for the care only of people with tuberculosis, often described as consumption.

For a while some physicians recommended cool damp ocean air for healing and others, the hot dry air of the desert. Fresh air in cities was in such demand that the heads of beds were placed outside the windows and the bottoms of these beds were secured inside the room. Inside those sickrooms, patients were not allowed out of bed but were told to rest. They waited in their beds for a new set of X-ray pictures that might show an improvement in their whitish covered lungs and offer hope that the disease was arrested.

Franklin Earle Burkett and Ethel Rae (Reichard) moved to Bethlehem, Pennsylvania about 30 miles from Oxford, New Jersey where Franklin had been born. He thought it best to take his wife there for a fresh start away from tuberculosis, the germs, and memories. Fortunately, work was available in the steel industry and its machine shops were looking for responsible employees who had a knack for working with their hands.

Their second baby, Charles Franklin, named after grandfather and father, was born on Valentine's Day in 1914 and Ethel Rae presented the infant to her husband instead of a lacy card with Cupid and arrows. She tried to forget her baby girl, Ruth, and claimed her tears were those of joy.

Two months later, grandpa Charles Stout Burkett died and he and his tuberculosis were carefully buried in Frenchtown Cemetery.

Meanwhile, the tall-case Burkett clock had been transported to the house in Bethlehem and with it a sense of continuity to the little family that had so recently lost their firstborn and a father, Charles Stout Burkett. In spite of the family losses, the Burkett annual celebration dinner on Thanksgiving 1915 was held in Flemington at the home of another Charles, the nephew of Charles S. and the grandson of the first Charles. It was such an impressive celebration, with family attending from all over New Jersey, that it made the local newspaper as if the Burketts were high society. Gratitude was the theme that year in keeping with giving thanks at this holiday and they all sang "blest be the ties that bind" with an impressive prayer offered up before disbanding.[5]

Little Charles was growing quickly and Ethel Rae found herself pregnant a third time. Dorothy Ethel was born in late February of 1918 and Ethel Rae was so busy taking care of the children that she had no time for anything except cooking and cleaning. But whenever she stopped to breathe, she looked at the Sunday New York Times. She saw horrors captured in the sepia photos of the rotogravure section and was saddened to the point of despair at the battle scenes. If Franklin hadn't been exempted from the draft, that is where he'd be now. The war was not going well.

Adding to the miseries of trench warfare, influenza was beginning to take hold all over the world. Bodies of sailors were being dumped at sea when they couldn't be buried properly on land. The topic of the pandemic was the subject of conversations everywhere. Ethel Rae didn't dare take little Charles and Dorothy

---

[5] News clipping from Hunterdon County Democrat, Flemington, NJ December 1, 1915

around people who might be sniffling or, god forbid, coughing.

Meanwhile, Franklin's factory had been overwhelmed with orders for war related equipment. He was happy, though also felt a little guilty, to be exempted from the army because of his employment in an industry critical to the war effort.

⟪◎

One cold November day in 1918 the Burkett's candlestick phone rang. It was a Mr. Jacoby, Chief of Police in Easton, Pennsylvania. He was saying something about Ethel Rae's father and a shooting.

Ethel Rae asked him to speak up because she couldn't understand a thing he was saying.

"Are you Ethel Rae Reichard Burkett?" Chief Jacoby repeated. When she answered yes, he began again, "Just a minute, please," and passed the phone to his detective. Another voice came on, "Detective Neimeyer here…I'm afraid we have very bad news for you."

Ethel Rae was impatient and still not certain they had the correct phone number. "Who are you? What is it…please. Speak louder." Chief Jacoby yelled into his end of the phone. "This is the Easton Police Department. Your father has shot himself to death. And he has killed Catherine, his wife."

A crackling silence came across the wires as though the line had gone dead, but Ethel Rae had hung up the earpiece in a daze to call Franklin at the factory to come straight home.

When he arrived an hour later, he found Ethel Rae scrubbing the face of the old tall-case clock. She was in another world with an empty look in her eyes, a look Franklin had never seen, as she methodically continued to wipe off all the black lettering inside the numbers. With a one track mind Ethel Rae then further attacked the remaining smudges. She was using Bab-O, an abrasive kitchen cleanser that she knew would erase forever the evil black letters on the sunny white face.

Ethel Rae was undoubtedly thinking about how she lost her mother when she was only 16 and had to go live with her Aunt Anna and later with her Uncle Earnest. And then her adorable baby Ruth died after Grandfather Burkett got her sick. Then Grandfather Burkett succumbed to his tuberculosis. And now her father was dead, horribly dead, by his own hand, and he'd taken along with him her stepmother, Catherine, who did not deserve to be shot in the face.

In her state of fresh grief Ethel Rae saw the day's horror as a continuation of the Schultz curse begun when her grandparents married after her mother was born.

Because August and Augusta were first cousins,[6] the young people were to be kept apart by convention in spite of their great love for each other. But like the rebellious Martin Luther, they did the unthinkable. They ran away to America and married. Nobody in the new country would suspect it was anything other than coincidence that they were named August and Augusta and had the same last names. And so they planned to live happily ever after.

Franklin gently wrestled the damp cloth away from the dry-eyed Ethel Rae who had begun to push the hands of the clock backwards toward 12:45. She would have been grateful had it still

[6] Their fathers were brothers

been yesterday and time had frozen prior to the gunshots.

Franklin picked up the bawling baby and handed her off to Ethel Rae who had collapsed on the sofa. The toddler, Charles, was sitting wide-eyed in a corner having never seen his mother in such an odd state.

The doctor came immediately while Ethel Rae fed her baby. He stirred 10 grains of barbitol into water for Ethel Rae to swallow.

⟪◎

It wasn't until the next morning when Ethel Rae had a chance to read the letter that her father, Jacob Lewis Reichard, had written immediately before taking her stepmother by taxi out toward the Raubsville power station along the Delaware Canal. He had dismissed the driver and they were on foot when witnesses heard the three gunshots. First he murdered Catherine and then killed himself. [7]

She then understood how out of touch she'd been. The depth of her father's agonizing depression was impossible to fathom. And how lost he must have felt in a pit so dark and filled with irrational thinking that he had an obsessive need to buy a .38 caliber pistol to end the lives of both Catherine and himself. Once he'd made up his mind, he couldn't turn back.

In the letter was a reference to his shame that Catherine was leaving him and this blow, stacked on top of the abandonment death of his beloved young first wife, was shattering. Jacob Lewis

---

[7] Easton Express-Argus, Tuesday, 12 November, 1918 page 1 "Killed Wife and Self" "J. Lewis Reichard Ended Two Lives With Bullets From a Revolver"

had no understanding of how Catherine could consider a move into a strange household 60 miles away from him. He wrote in the note he was refusing to allow her to leave. And moreover, it was all her fault that she wouldn't empathize sufficiently with his money woes and everything else that was wrong with his life.

An insane war raged inside of Jacob Lewis Reichard although in the outside world, the armistice between Germany and the United States had been signed exactly one day before.[8]

⟪☙

While the world began to breathe again, it wasn't until Jacob Lewis and Catherine Reichard were buried that a semblance of normalcy returned for Franklin and Ethel Rae. It was only then that Franklin recognized how upset he was by his wife's assault on his clock, the bought-with-butter clock that kept precision time for him, a steady metronome to the various rhythms of his life. While he understood she wasn't in her right mind after she heard the dreadful news of the deaths, Franklin still found it impossible to let go his devotion to the sanctity of the old clock. He'd treated it like a shrine as he often removed the hood to admire its inner workings. But now the face was gray as it mirrored the sad state of mind of Ethel Rae.

So when Franklin had a chance to move to Plainfield, New Jersey to work for Walter Scott and Company shortly after the tragedy, he jumped at the chance to get closer to his roots. The family moved to 1332 Belleview a short walk to Walter Scott and Company where he was a machinist and very particular about the

---

[8] Author's footnote: Was Jacob's personal shame somehow conflated with the absolute German shame imposed by the harsh terms of complete surrender?

quality of his work. As a gentle man, Franklin was not especially happy that the company had orders for guns for the military, but he was relieved to have left the shadows of memories of the old neighborhood.

Franklin often stayed late at work to fiddle around with precision tools used for printing presses. He thought he could have been a jeweler or a clockmaker because he had a deft and sure touch. One night, he surprised Ethel Rae with a pendant for her birthday. He'd fashioned the piece from old gold and two new pearls, welding and bending it into a perfectly proportioned and delicate triangle with sharp points but softened by circles of eternal life. Presenting it to Ethel Rae accomplished much more than Franklin expected and provided her a distraction from her mourning for her own losses and those of mothers all around her whose sons would not be coming home from the battles of the Great War or the cruelty of the influenza pandemic.

❧

Franklin always tried to do the right thing and worked hard to cheer up Ethel Rae. He often suggested they ask his mother, Jennie, to watch the children so they could go to the movies to see Mary Pickford, the girl with the curls, or Charlie Chaplin in his latest movie. Most of the time, Ethel Rae said no and made an excellent case for being tired or staying home in light of the continued prevalence of influenza. In her heart, Ethel wasn't so tired as she was afraid of illness and not in the mood to watch Charlie Chaplin or Buster Keaton romping on top of trains or surviving explosions in daredevil style. Neither was she anxious to see Mary Pickford dressed up like Little Lord Fauntleroy. Still, she wasn't unhappy that her Franklin had contributed to Mary Pickford's $10,000 per week earnings by buying her some Mary Pickford spoons.

Franklin Burkett, a toolmaker for 25 years with Walter Scott and Co., died at home on December 7, 1951 at age 69 after a long illness. He was a member of the Methodist Church in Plainfield, New Jersey and was buried in New Cemetery in Somerville, New Jersey.

Ethel Rae and Franklin's bought-with-butter clock moved in with their son, Charles Franklin and his wife, Jeanne Schoenbaum, in 1962. Ethel Rae never again touched the face of the clock.

FIFTH GENERATION
Charles Franklin Burkett
February 14, 1914 – October 11, 1994

Charles Franklin Burkett was a safety engineer with Westinghouse and was a quiet man and a thinker. He could fix things and was known to have hammered together a perfect set of porch steps as though they were a simple jigsaw puzzle. His wife, Jeanne Schoenbaum Burkett (October 22, 1910 - October 20, 2002), was said to have been a gourmet cook.

Charles had little contact with extended family except through correspondence and occasional three-minute phone calls with his sister Dorothy Ethel Burkett Warrington who lived in another state with her husband, Ralph Malcolm Warrington, Jr. and their four children. He and Jeanne had no children and no one knows whether they didn't want to bring children into a terrifying world that suffered the hunger of the Depression, the miseries of World War II, and the murder of the Lindbergh baby that occurred less than an hour from their home, or if their God just never made it happen. The couple did attend church regularly and possibly prayed one way or the other about having children.[9]

The couple moved to Interhaven Street in North Plainfield, New Jersey because Jeanne had grown up on the top of the hill and loved to play up in the clouds as a child. Happy memories enticed her back to that place with air so pure that injured veterans were brought to the hill to relax amidst the healing properties of nature. The Burkett's house itself was small and poorly insulated with no visible forces of feng shui to create harmony unless one factored in the aromas from Jeanne's kitchen and the dependable sounds of the tall-case clock. The steep stairs to the second floor stood directly across a tiny entry hall from the front door and led to the bathroom on the second floor. And the clock fit nicely into the back sunroom where the smudged face looked a little brighter than when it lived in the Franklin Earle and Ethel Rae living room.

One fine day in June after Charles and Jeanne had died, their ashes were scattered on their hill in a Boy Scout-like outing orchestrated by Jeanne's niece, Phyllis Schoenbaum Lange, the executrix of her Aunt Jeanne's estate. The respectful group cautiously made its way to the top of the hill and sprinkled what remained of Charles and Jeanne over their beloved hillside.

---

[9] It is suspected that Charles was disappointed that he didn't have a son. Instead, he threw himself into his work as a scout leader with the Boy Scouts of America.

⟨ℚ

Phyllis Schoenbaum Lange, became a modern day heroine for the Burkett/Warrington family because of her determination to do the right thing. Just as in the generations past, the clock's custodians always did the right thing to safeguard the clock. Phyllis somehow had the courage and presence of mind to transfer the clock to a stranger whom she'd never met. For her, the clock was far more valuable than a 200-year-old mahogany case that housed an ingenious and delicately balanced mechanism. The clock represented the Burkett family history and she knew that it didn't belong to her.

Phyllis had bought the little house at 30 Interhaven from the Charles and Jeanne Burkett Estate and knew early on from discussions with her aunt that the clock was to be delivered "when the time came" to the oldest son in the Burkett line. She was determined to follow her aunt's wishes and immediately changed the locks on the house in order to protect the clock from disappearing into the back room of an antiques dealer.

SIXTH GENERATION
Ralph Malcolm Warrington, III
April 28, 1943...

Ralph is the oldest nephew of Charles Franklin Burkett and is very much a Burkett in his ingenuity, calm demeanor, competence and easy laugh, not to mention his aquiline nose. He is a civil engineer whose career designing and constructing offshore platforms for Shell Oil Company sent him from Alaska to Australia, from Japan and Korea to London. His wife, Freda Spector Warrington, and his family of a son and daughter, accompanied him in company transfers from California, to Louisiana, to Texas, and back to California. He retired to Saratoga Springs, New York and Sarasota, Florida.

The clock is unstressed and dusted carefully in the Warrington's home as it waits to be transferred to their son, Daniel Alden Warrington, and after him, his son, Rocco Max Warrington.

⟨ℚ

When the clock's present caretaker, Ralph Malcolm Warrington, III, looks at the Spencer and Nolen painted dial with the smudge where the clockmaker's name was Babo'd off, he's reminded of shattered lives of pain and suffering. When he sees the short ball feet, he's reminded that someone lopped off the skirted base of the clock for personal reasons that he'll never know. When he notes the small box with key and wrench, it's apparent that the clock was beloved across the centuries. This clock offers ample evidence that just living is a mixed bag of good and evil, sadness and joy.

Phyllis guessed correctly that if the clock had eyes, ears, and the gift of speech rather than a set of chimes, it could tell a whopper of a story. Not only did it stand within range of the family radio to hear the shocking details about the Lindbergh kidnapping, murder, and trial over in the Flemington Courthouse, it heard Victrola foxtrots for the young people to practice their flapper dancing. It overheard arguments over whether the so-called science of eugenics that Hitler subscribed to was the creation of

America or the extremist actions of one insane man.

While the clock continues to measure time in a one-second-at-a-time, micro manner, it ultimately hovers above history and culture. Its spread is larger than the sum of its seconds and minutes, with a purpose that is at present mostly metaphorical.

Its treasure rests in family history, both revealed and imagined, floating as it has over two centuries of Burketts. Some of them were religious Lutherans, Presbyterians, Baptists, and Methodists and many others, not so religious and positively rebellious. All were shrewd at times although sometimes not so clever and fit the description of normal human beings.

Every family is a repository for secrets and a catalyst for tensions to develop, but a family also offers respite and comfort after tragedy. This Burkit/Burkett family was no different, devastated as it was by the death of an infant child and grown children, a murder and a suicide, early deaths, and the scourge of tuberculosis that took at least three family members. But throughout these crises, the Burkett tall-case clock stood to bind father to son and generation to generation until it landed with its present custodian for the rest of his time on earth.

Ralph Malcolm Warrington III didn't arrive in this world, as he believed, in the vacuum of a small and safe nuclear family. The clock's history has proven that beyond a shadow of a doubt. With a new and expanded vision he now takes his place on the branch of an ancestral tree discovered in the history of the old clock. He might have preferred a castle, but in its absence he opens the glass in front of the dial and looks closely, time and again, hoping to see the smudges more distinctly. Or he unlocks the front door of the case to check on the pendulum and then draws up the weights. Is he looking for another secret, a scrap of old paper or an undiscovered pencil marking? Or is he beginning to get attached to that old Heppelwhite high style East New Jersey tall-case clock with its three proud brass finials? Is he taking pride in his personal spot within history and the context of the Burkett family?

Serious questions remain about the wisdom of a genealogic snoop tacking on documented facts to what otherwise might have been a far more romantic imagined backstory to accompany the clock. Its present and future caretakers would otherwise have been able to plug in pleasant historic possibilities without the cluttering truths.

Might the secrets and tragedies uncovered in researching the clock's history be better left undiscovered and scattered into cold blizzard winds or over the loose dirt of the graves of the babies… or the murdered? Or, among the ashes of Charles and Jeanne? Is it wanton hubris of the sixth generation, with all of its digitized information, that allows a seemingly gratuitous voyeurism to peer into the sleeping past? Or is it a valid rationale that the clock's history, good and bad, exists as an anchor, a taproot, for its latest caretakers?

Is it too late to rebury the clock's history or may we rationalize the intrusion by promising not to make judgments? And awful to consider—will the seventh and eighth generations wonder why they would need or want to keep the clock when smart phones in our pockets tell us the time and everything else?

HOUSEKEEPING

Dr. David Sperling, a tall-case clock expert, can only guess that the clock was made by George Rea, Richard Hooley, Joakim Hill or even another New Jersey clockmaker. Because Ethel Rae Reichard Burkett scrubbed off the name on the face of the clock, we will never know for certain the name of the clockmaker without a forensic intervention. The author has taken literary license in assigning the clock to Richard Hooley due to the proximity of his shop to John Burkit's church in the early 19th century.

The Author thanks the following people for reviewing the story: Joyce Radochia, Ann Roecker, Alisa Fisher, Alfred Spector, David Colman, and Ralph Warrington, III.

Documents from the Hall of Records' County Clerk's Office, Hunterdon County, New Jersey for the Burkit/Burket/Burkett property in Kingwood Township detailed two parcels of land owned by John Burkit that were transferred to Charles Burkit and Sylvester Burkit in 1856 when John was about 83 years old. John's wife, Mary Fox, had died at age 55.

Sylvester then deeded his share of the property on April 2, 1862 to his brother, Charles, for $2600.

Charles Burkett died in 1887 and his executors were his oldest son, Thomas P. Burkett and his son-in-law, Jeremiah H. Rittenhouse. They both died before executing the will and Mary Elizabeth Burkett Rittenhouse, the widow of Jeremiah and daughter of Charles, along with their son, Judson B. Rittenhouse, became the executors. They were empowered by the will to sell the property and did so after the death of Nancy Housel Burkett.

Mary Elizabeth Burkett Rittenhouse had bought the property at auction for $122 on October 14, 1902 at that time.

Henry C. Roberson bought the property in July of 1913 after it had been in the Burkett family since the 1700s.

The tall-case clock bought with butter in 1805 went its separate way and moved in with Charles Stout Burkett, the fourth and living son of Charles Burkett. Then, it went to live with his son, Franklin Earle Burkett. Next it was given to his son Charles Franklin Burkett and after the death of his wife, it landed in the 21st century at the home of Charles Franklin Burkett's nephew, Ralph Malcolm Warrington, III. (His mother was Dorothy Ethel Burkett Warrington, younger sister to Charles Franklin Burkett.) The clock is promised next to Daniel Alden Warrington (November 6, 1972...) and then to Daniel's son, Rocco Max Warrington (November 13, 2006...).

Acknowledgments

I'm grateful to the dearest friend of my life, Joyce Hepburn Radochia. She's the Joy in "The Samovar and the Egg" and has been and remains my constant cheerleader. Since no one yet has written the definitive book on the subject of friendship, she and I continue to plot and plan.

My girlfriends have been blessings along the accidental paths I've traveled, none of them planned. My childhood friendships are memorable for their ease as we reconfigured our twosomes, threesomes, and foursomes. We wasted a lot of time together at hockey games, hanging around Harvard Square looking to pick up college boys, and cutting and pasting the <u>Arlington High School Chronicle</u>. I mostly survived the Vassar ivory tower experience intact due to the willing availability of my college girlfriends and Joyce (always Joyce) who was with me most of the time. I learned from each and every one of them although I dare not say exactly what I learned.

Former roommate, Dr. Judy Saide, offered a break after college stress and during the days I worked full time and went to library school full time. She retains her hearty laugh and is a gifted teacher to me and to her students. Phyllis remains a standout for her steady loyalty and patience.

During my lonely New Orleans days and nights as a terrified new mom to two kids and when my husband was offshore more than onshore, I hung on by a thread with Martha Brasted, my trusted alter ego, and the capable Susan Sterling, ready to catch me. The late Gail Hopkins tried to teach me how to craft, crochet, and decoupage after we came home each day from teaching public school, but I was a hopeless student. My landlady, another Joyce, taught me how to cook, serve, and eat crabs, crayfish, and shrimp as well as how to find tickets and dress properly to watch a Mardi Gras ball. MaryAnn taught me what Audubon Drive and caviar look like and then graciously invited us along to her parties.

In Kingwood, Texas I found Honey in the contemporary corner house, the incomparable Carol Appelbaum, my one Jewish friend in the community, Mary Arnold, and the late Sue Womack, all of whom were essential neighbors who would kill snakes for me and drive me to the hospital when one of my kids broke his collarbone. We played bridge and tennis, complained, hung out at the duck pond, shared gourmet recipes, worried and watched each other's children. In hindsight I could be describing a bunch of ne'er-do-well hangers-on, but we were totally dedicated to the wellbeing of our children and worked hard at parenting.

My Saturday morning Grupo girlfriends in Bakersfield, California, Dianne, Joan, Sally, Amy, Judy, Dinah, and Brenda were trusted with serious secrets. Imagine being able to reveal anything and everything in Joan's office and never suffer a breach of confidentiality? We could have run the CIA and then solved all the problems of the world, given enough time and tissues.

During my Central Valley years I had a serious walking friendship (we were addicted to talking), music teacher friends, and a baklava friend. My colleagues at work offered me courage to continue in a new direction as director of chemical dependency treatment at the satellite office of a psychiatric hospital. Claire,

Barbara Ann, Susie, whom I hired to help me along, my bosses Diane and Judy, and my supervisor, the late Dr. Marilyn Browning, along with my interns and Jan H., welcomed me to the real world "out there." Having them all as mentors was a lucky break for me.

In Newport Beach, California where I spent the happiest days of my life I found a big sister, Alice Remer, to advise me. She was a soft-spoken Phi Beta Kappa girl who knew just about everything. My Bat Yahm Sisterhood book club members, all of whom I love to this day, were consistently on deck. The late Ellie (Hands) Burg, Leslea, Linda O., Linda F., another extraordinary Joyce, Ann our linear thinker, Judy, Sharon, Marj and Elaine have read together for so long and express a depth of insight into the literature that blows me away. Thanks especially to Leslea for not blackballing me during my phone chat interview, as well to the others for integrating me so willlingly into their established group.

The girlfriends who come in and out of my life are always welcome and honored: Helen, Haia, Pnina, Suzanne, Beryl, Win, Jan, Bonnie, Judy, Virginia, Hope, Peggy, Regina, Cousins Bette, Linda, Roberta and Debi and sister-in-law and queen of home arts, Michiko.

I am thankful for the inspiration of my newest friends, the energetic Dr. Joyce Robinson and the can-do Harrilyn Beehner, as well as the late Dr. Joel Elkes whom I did not meet until he was 100 years old. It was Dr. Joel's unusual, intense, and intelligent gaze that prompted me to understand what he meant when he advised us all to "listen to the light."

Thanks to my serious readers: Dr. Hermione de Almeida, David Colman, Phyllis Jansen, Dianne Cooper, Dr. Sylvia Feinberg,

Beryl Ruff, Susan Jacobs, Sybil Goldman, storyteller Frannie Oates, Dr. Alfred Spector, my British girlfriend, the other Freda Warrington ("Doppleganger"), as well as the talented Random House editor, Andy Ward, who has written positive commentary and encouraged my writing.

I'm beyond grateful to our daughter, Alisa Fisher, for her wise counsel and complete honesty. My late mother, Ethel Etta Karelitz Spector, led the way for me by insisting that every woman needed something more in her life. For her the "more" was her law degree and love of the law. For me it is my love for simple stories—other people's and my own. I recognize the complexity of our lives in them.

My great appreciation goes to Phyllis Lange who made certain the Burkett tall case clock was returned to my husband ("Bought With Butter").

Thanks to Austin Metze for his exquisite cover and design expertise and to Chris Angermann for bringing this book to completion.

Finally, loving thanks go to my husband of 50 years, Ralph Malcolm Warrington, III, for allowing me to pursue anything and everything that makes me happy.

Biography

Freda Spector Warrington grew up in Arlington, Massachusetts and received her bachelor's degree from Vassar College. She studied library science at Simmons, education at LSU and Tulane, and counseling at Cal State, Bakersfield. She was an editor, a public school teacher and a piano instructor, and spent most of her career in the health care industry.

She was in charge of outpatient addiction recovery programs in a psychiatric hospital clinic and served as Executive Director of Healthy Mothers, Healthy Babies of Kern County, a collaborative that addressed high infant mortality and morbidity in California's Central Valley. She also was project director for a federal CSAP collaborative grant for Kern County, worked as a consultant for California Women's Commission on Addictions providing trainings and technical assistance, and was past President of Orange Coast Interfaith Shelter's Friends Board. In addition, she supervised substance abuse treatment programs both for Native Americans and for people with developmental disabilities.

Freda is married to Ralph Warrington, a retired project manager for Shell Oil Company. They have two children, Daniel Warrington and Alisa Fisher, and six grandchildren.

For more information and group discussion questions please go to:
www.FredaSWarrington.com